Practically Project Management

A Resource for Everyday Project Managers

by Jon Hanley, MBA, PMP

practicallyproject.com

ISBN: 9798851023163

First edition July 2023.

This book is independently published by practically project management. To contact us visit: practicallyproject.com

DEDICATION

First and foremost, this book is dedicated to my wife Denise and my daughters Elizabeth and Gwyneth. You've been right by my side every step of the way. In good times and in not so good times. You're the reason I do what I do.

Secondly, I want to dedicate this book to my parents for their support and inspiration. I am truly blessed. My passion for projects is because of you.

Finally, I would like to dedicate this book to my colleagues, managers, teachers, and mentors who have challenged and supported me over the years. I would especially like to thank the leaders who took a chance on me when no one else would – you know who you are. This book is a result of the experiences I've had working alongside each and every one of you.

CONTENTS

ACKNOWLEDGMENT

This book represents years of compiling personal notes, short essays, and blog posts on topics related to project management, product management, innovation, technology, shared services, marketing, business, and careers. It began based on things I was passionate about, yet it didn't have a consistent flow.

Without the resources to employ a professional copy editor or designers, I had always assumed that this book would never be published.

However, with the assistance of AI tools, I was finally able to assemble my content into a cohesive book format with a reasonable amount of effort. I would like to thank the team at OpenAI for providing the editing tools that made it possible for me to publish this book.

The book's cover was crafted by Abdul Halim. Even though he was halfway around the world from me, we were able to collaborate seamlessly via the Upwork platform. My sincere thanks to Abdul for working through multiple iterations of the design and the team at Upwork for creating such an easy-to-use platform for getting work done.

The images on each section page were obtained from a variety of photographers on the royalty-free image site Pixabay. Credit for each artist is highlighted at the bottom of those pages.

WHY READ THIS BOOK

"Does the world need another book about project management?" This is a question that has weighed heavily on my mind. After engaging in deep introspection, I identified two crucial aspects that I wanted to address through this book.

Firstly, it struck me that while project management is a ubiquitous skill, it is not practically taught in schools. Consider this: at some point in our lives, everyone is called upon to lead a project. These endeavors often do not involve the complexities of launching a spaceship or spearheading groundbreaking technological innovations. They are everyday undertakings such as organizing a special event, establishing a small business, or enhancing a workplace process. Yet, there is a common assumption that everyone possesses the inherent skills and knowledge to effectively lead a project without being taught.

Secondly, I have always found project management to be one of the most exhilarating fields, but unfortunately, most project management materials are uninspiring and tedious to read. They typically fall into two categories: overly academic treatises or mere sales pitches for proprietary methods that offer nothing new. In both cases, the available content fails to resonate with the majority of people, thereby depriving them of valuable insights.

It is these realizations that served as the catalyst for writing this book. My aim was to create a resource that is practical, accessible, and brimming with real-life examples, effectively bridging the gap between specialized resources utilized by project management professionals and the everyday projects or situations where individuals may need guidance.

To achieve this goal, I have organized the book into distinct sections that feature personal stories, practical examples, and simple templates. Whether you prefer reading it cover to cover or referring to specific topics related to a particular challenge, I'm confident this book will accommodate your needs.

FOR THE LOVE OF PROJECT MANAGEMENT

My father, just like my grandfather, was a building contractor in a small town in Ohio. Despite what OSHA guidelines permit, I spent much of my childhood at construction sites. It seems like just yesterday when I was looking over the dashboard of my dad's rusted Ford pickup truck with empty pouches of Workhorse brand chewing tobacco strewn across the seats. While other little kids played in their sandboxes with toy trucks, I went to construction sites with real bulldozers and dump trucks.

I was fascinated with construction because people always created, fixed, or improved something. Everything was solid and real. When the work was complete, it somehow felt like the world was a little bit better. To this day, I still get sentimental whenever I catch the smell of fresh-cut lumber or damp earth that has been dug up.

Fast forward about 30 years. There I was, a Sr. Director of an enterprise project management office (ePMO) at a 50 billion dollar company looking outside my office window. I had indeed achieved success in my career as a business professional. That's when I started reflecting on my journey. I had come a long way from being a little kid wandering around a construction site. In the blink of an eye, I completed business school, obtained a master's degree, and led countless project assignments that took my family and me all over the world. In this moment of reflection, I broke out in quiet laughter. I realized what they say is true; we all turn into our parents. Despite how different my career path had been, unbeknownst to myself, I still ended up following in the footsteps of my father and grandfather. While they were called building contractors, they were actually project managers. They designed plans, scoped the work, estimated and financed jobs, organized teams, fought with sub-contractors, fired deadbeats, stepped up to solve problems, and constantly adjusted plans to meet the changing demands of their customers. These were the same activities I was leading, but instead of being surrounded by piles of lumber and bricks, I was surrounded by piles of paper, computer code, and grey cubicles.

It was in this moment of clarity that it dawned on me. <u>I loved project management.</u> Regardless of the project, you can look at the fruits of your labor and feel the pure unadulterated joy of accomplishment. It doesn't matter if it's building a house or coding software. Completing a project just feels good. And when you're done, there's inevitably another challenge waiting just around the corner. That's what makes project management so unique. That's why I love project management.

My hope is the content in this book sparks a similar love for projects and equips you with new insights to overcome the daily challenges that face every one of us.

I intend to continue producing updated versions of this book based on new experiences, insights, and feedback that I receive. If you have suggestions, criticisms, or just want to drop a note to say hello, you can reach me via the contact page at practicallyproject.com. **<u>Thank You</u>** for buying this book.

SECTION 1

The Essential Tools of Project Management

Every project is characterized by its uniqueness, presenting infinite possibilities for how the work is accomplished. Whether it involves building a towering skyscraper or creating a sophisticated software application, there exist fundamental methods that enable successful project completion. Similar to a skilled craftsman distinguishing between a wrench and a screwdriver, effective project management starts with acquiring knowledge of proven tools and methodologies essential for achieving project objectives.

[Image by Pexels from Pixabay]

The 10 Tools of Effective Project Management

At one point in my career I managed a team of over 50 project managers who were responsible for overseeing more than 200 projects of various sizes. Additionally, I had oversight for about twice as many contractors. One of the key challenges I faced as a leader was providing consistent direction among a diverse range of styles, situations, and project types that we encountered on a daily basis. Unfortunately, I often found myself entangled in the quagmire of conflicting project management approaches advocated by different individuals.

Like many executives, I was bombarded with cold calls from high-priced consultants who pitched training programs and the latest technology platforms promising to "transform" my project management teams. Yet, it seemed that with each new initiative, we only added unnecessary complexity that hindered our progress. In the midst of this daily chaos, I became fixated on the idea that things should be simpler.

One day, fed up with the situation, I sat in my office reviewing our project list and pondered a fundamental question: "Why do some projects succeed while others fail?" and "Are there common factors that contribute to project success or failure?"

Determined to find answers, I embarked on a mission that involved attending numerous project review meetings and spending countless hours observing project teams while asking probing questions. I meticulously cross-referenced industry benchmarks, delved into project management reference guides, and compared them to our own project practices. Here is what I discovered:

1. A significant portion of teams claimed to follow specific project management methodologies, but *approximately 50% of them were not truly adhering to these methodologies*. When I requested examples of required artifacts, they often couldn't

provide them. Some teams used the excuse of "agile methodology" to justify doing things their own way, while others used "waterfall methodology" to justify sluggishness or neglecting dependencies with other teams. Some even outright stated that their project sponsors didn't consider methodologies necessary, dismissing them as mere "busy work."

2. There was a *lack of a common language or culture* among different project managers. Expectations varied widely based on their previous work experiences, educational backgrounds, and organizational origins.

3. The most successful teams were those that *fostered regular meetings, shared common goals, established clear metrics, and maintained open lines of communication*. The specific project management methodology used was secondary, as they always found ways to collaborate effectively.

Armed with these insights, I took action. However, as any business leader knows, implementing significant changes within established organizations is an incredibly difficult task. Even when change is possible, the execution can be complex, costly, and yield mixed results. Effecting widespread behavioral change necessitates focus and simplicity.

Herein lies the catch-22 of elaborate training programs, proprietary methods, and sophisticated project management technology platforms. While they may be technically "correct" on their own, they often prove ineffective in the real world. By the time they are implemented, a new approach surfaces, tempting someone to believe it's better for their team or organization.

Basketball legend Michael Jordan said, "The minute you get away from fundamentals – whether it's proper technique, work ethic, or mental preparation – the bottom can fall out of your game, your schoolwork, your job, or whatever you're doing."

With this wisdom in mind, rather than relying on external consultants, I assembled an "All-Star" team comprising our best project managers to collectively identify the primary tools necessary for project success. **The fundamentals**. This proved challenging, as everyone held strong opinions. However, after a vigorous debate, we agreed upon "10 tools" that were essential for every project.

We refined these tools, printed them on a single sheet of paper, shared exemplary instances, provided training, and set the expectation that individuals would be held accountable for their application.

The checklist of 10 fundamental tools is as follows:

1. A **project charter** with a clearly defined scope or prioritized list of deliverables.
2. Measurable **success criteria**.
3. A project **organization model** that outlines roles, responsibilities, and reporting relationships.
4. A **decision-making process** for the project team to approve changes to scope, budget, and staffing.
5. A minimum weekly **status report** to facilitate communication with stakeholders.
6. A **project plan**, aligned with the declared methodology, highlighting deliverable deadlines.
7. A **budget management** process illustrating the overall budget and its current status.
8. A **communication plan** to manage change within the internal organization and external customer relationships.
9. A **risk and issue tracking** list, with assigned owners and specified resolution deadlines.

10. A declared **project management methodology** to guide the work, with an expectation that the team can produce necessary artifacts.

That's it. Ten "tools" distilled down to approximately 130 words. Accountability was straightforward, as anyone could audit a project using the 10-item checklist. The expectations were so basic that anyone could apply them to their projects. It was up to each individual to determine the best way to utilize them within their unique circumstances and identify any additional tools or approaches they deemed necessary.

In the book's first section, we will explore each of these tools and provide practical insights on their application.

Project Charters: Setting Clear Expectations

Once I worked as a computer programmer with responsibility for programming and configuring a small section of an extensive enterprise resource planning (ERP) system. This system was intricately integrated into almost every aspect of the company.

Within the programming team, there was one particularly unique individual. Some might even describe him as eccentric. Despite holding a director-level position, he had no direct reports, a rarity within the company. What's more, every afternoon at around 1:30 pm, he would hang a "Do Not Disturb" sign on his office door and indulge in a one-hour nap. No one dared to disturb his slumber. But here's the twist: he also adamantly refused to attend any management meetings, considering them an utter waste of his time and talents. Other managers would occasionally grumble, but they left him to his own devices as he performed two essential functions:

1. Training people on proper system programming.
2. Reviewing, editing, and approving every single line of custom code before it entered the system.

In essence, if you were a programmer, your code would never go live without his review and approval. However, he only examined code under two conditions:

1. If it was related to a training class he taught.
2. If it was associated with an officially chartered project.

Let that sink in for a moment. If a manager requested a minor system modification that wasn't part of an officially chartered project, it would not happen unless it was an emergency fix. His rationale was clear and calculated: if a change wasn't significant enough to warrant official written sponsorship, it was akin to the pointless management meetings he shunned—a complete waste of his time and talent. To this day, I'm convinced this man was a genius.

This scenario is all too familiar in virtually every organization, regardless of its size or industry. The demand for work consistently outweighs the available resources. Consequently, when work isn't prioritized, people tend to tackle whatever tasks come their way, even if they are trivial. This lack of focus and effectiveness undermines the potential of many organizations. Enter the project charter—an invaluable solution to this issue. It acts as a filter, allowing high-priority work to shine while limiting low-priority tasks.

It's unsurprising that many individuals scoff at the notion of chartering projects. They find it inconvenient to assess their requests within the context of broader organizational priorities. The most common excuse is that project charters are bureaucratic and time-consuming. However, from my experience, it's often rooted in the fear that their pet project will be deprioritized or simply laziness in preparing a concise request. In practice, a project charter shouldn't take more than 30 minute to draft.

Here's all you need for a robust project charter:

1. A clear description of the project or **deliverable**.
2. An explanation of **why** the project is necessary.
3. An approximation of the **resources required** to complete it.
4. An **overview of the team** and the roles of team members.
5. An estimate of the project's **duration**.
6. Identification of the individual or group approving or **sponsoring the work**.
7. An assessment of **potential risks** involved.

These items form the core features of most charters. Additional elements may be added to adapt to specific methodologies, industries, or processes. However, the essence remains the same—setting clear expectations and prioritizing work effectively.

Measuring for Success: Evaluating Project Outcomes

There's something about a car wreck that captivates our attention. No matter who you are, when you come across an accident on the side of the road, you can't help but turn your head and look. While I'm no expert in psychology, I believe that a few thoughts cross the minds of most people in such situations:

1. I hope no one was injured.
2. I'm relieved it didn't happen to me.
3. Was it purely chance, or is there a lesson to be learned to avoid a similar fate?

In the realm of project management, a failed product launch can be likened to a car crash—a spectacle that captures our attention. Just take a moment to reflect, and you'll likely recall some memorable product failures. Personally, my top five list includes:

- WOW potato chips with Olestra
- New Coke
- Febreeze Scent Stories
- Microsoft Clippy
- Gerber Single Serve Jars for Adults

What baffles me the most about these failed product launches is that some of the most reputable companies in the world were behind them. Microsoft, Coca-Cola, Procter & Gamble, and Frito Lay, known for employing top talent from renowned universities, had their fair share of missteps. It's puzzling to contemplate how, at some point, a highly trained and handsomely compensated executive decided that consumers would want to buy potato chips with a warning label stating, "this product may cause abdominal cramping and loose stools."

While each failed product launch has its unique circumstances, two fundamental truths remain:

1. Someone delivered the project.
2. The launch was unsuccessful.

These simple facts underscore an often overlooked aspect of project management. Merely delivering a project on time, within budget, and as per the defined scope does not guarantee its success. True success is only achieved when the intended benefits are realized.

This realization presents a challenge for every project manager. Metrics for delivery, such as time, budget, and scope, primarily provide backward-looking insights into the project's progress and are thus easier to evaluate. On the other hand, project benefits are typically realized in the future and are more challenging to predict. However, just because something is difficult doesn't mean it's impossible or not worth pursuing. That's why I advocate for the inclusion of two general types of measures in most projects. I refer to them as:

1. **Delivery Quality Metrics (DQM):** These metrics focus on the "How" of project execution. They serve as process indicators, assessing the team's progress concerning time, budget, scope, and other factors that ensure successful delivery.
2. **Launch Quality Metrics (LQM):** These metrics center around the "Why" of project initiation. They evaluate whether the project is on track or has achieved its intended benefits. These often include things like sales, profit, adoption, satisfaction, process improvement indicators, etc.

By adopting <u>both</u> DQM and LQM, project managers can gain a comprehensive understanding of a project's performance and its alignment with the desired outcomes. While DQM helps ensure that you get the work done efficiently, LQM helps ensure you don't crash.

Project Organizations and Decision Making

Mark Twain once stated, "Humor is the good-sided nature of truth." Interestingly, my mother possessed both a great sense of humor and a talent for uncovering the truth. I vividly recall a small laminated sign she displayed in her office, which humorously depicted the 6 stages of a project:

1. Enthusiasm
2. Disillusionment
3. Panic
4. Search for the Guilty
5. Punishment of the Innocent
6. Praise and Honors for the Non-Participants

It was only later in life that the profound truth behind that amusing sign became evident. In contrast to projects resulting in the "punishment of the innocent," I have discovered three factors that minimize the chances of a project veering off course. While they may lack humor, they are undeniably accurate. These factors include:

1. A solid project premise
2. Deep insights about your customer or problem
3. Excellent execution

While a project manager may not always have control over the project premise or customer insights that initiated the project, they hold the power to ensure the effort is executed with excellence. And exceptional execution begins with organizing the project team.

The great news is that you are already an expert at team organization, even if you're unaware of it. My first experience in organizing teams dates back to grade school when we played soccer or football. Two individuals would take charge and select players based on their skills in particular positions. For instance, Jimmy is a talented defender, or Sally is remarkably fast. Defining your project team is as straightforward as that.

Just like a schoolyard football team cannot win without a capable quarterback, your project's success hinges on having the right people in the right roles. It is crucial to invest time in defining the required roles for the project and identifying suitable individuals to fill them. Document these roles and share them with the team, ensuring everyone understands their expectations. If certain positions cannot be filled, collaborate with others to find a solution. Additionally, if critical roles lack available personnel, consider it a risk to the project's delivery and communicate it accordingly.

For more complex projects, further clarification may be necessary regarding team organization. While some project managers employ the RASCI method, I prefer a simplified approach called PACE. PACE is an acronym representing:

- **Process Owner**
- **Approver**
- **Contributor**
- **Executor**

PACE serves as a decision-making model applicable to any project team. It is commonly employed in organization charts and decision matrices to ensure clarity regarding roles and responsibilities. Moreover, it aids in establishing how decisions are made when changes or guidance are required. An example of a basic project team chart illustrating the application of PACE is highlighted on the next page.

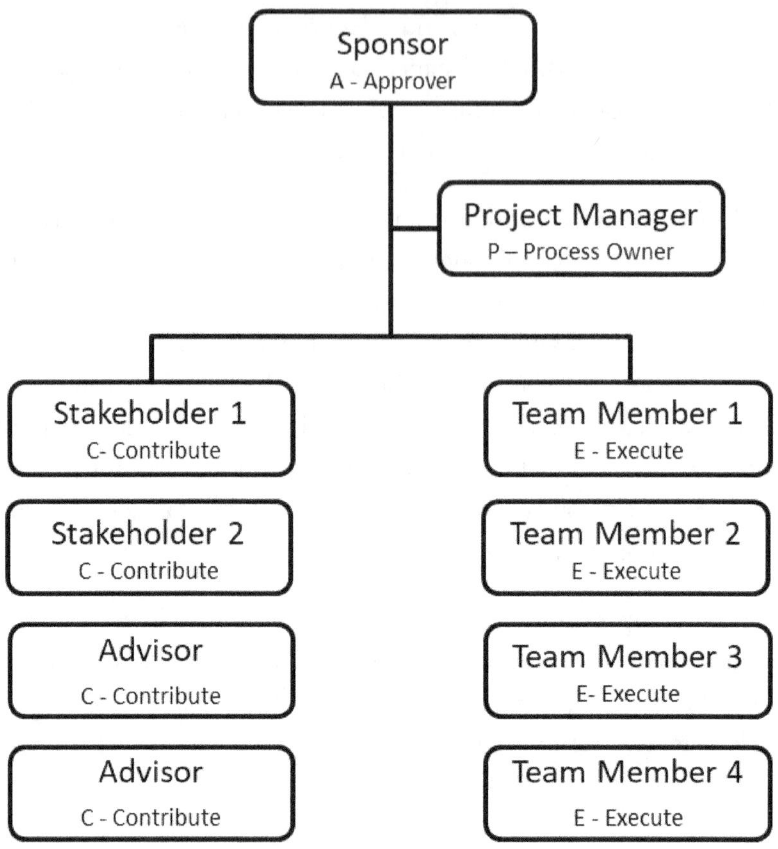

When designating the approver for a project, challenges may arise in highly matrixed organizations, as different departments may control resources. For instance, while the project sponsor might be from the marketing department, finance might need to approve or release funding, and project team members or the project owner may originate from the PMO or another division. In such cases, correctly defining the "approver" becomes even more critical. It may be necessary to determine who, apart from the immediate sponsor, ultimately holds the authority to make final decisions.

Once the approver is identified and empowered to allocate or withhold resources, attention shifts to the process owner. While the project manager usually fulfills this role, additional clarification may be necessary for multifunctional projects or large-scale programs involving multiple individuals.

Following clarity on the approver and process owner, the next step involves identifying contributors. These individuals may have strong opinions or offer valuable input, but they are not responsible for day-to-day work or decision-making authority. Be cautious, as senior-level contributors may be mistaken for approvers. It is crucial to differentiate these roles to minimize confusion.

Finally, there are the individuals who execute the work. Defining these roles is typically easier since they are accountable for delivering specific outcomes or performing necessary functions to complete the project.

To further illustrate the use of PACE, an example of an organizational model for a typical wedding is highlighted on the next page.

PACE	Resource
Approver	Bride
Process Owner	Wedding Planner
Contributor	Groom
Contributor	Mother of the Bride
Contributor	Father of the Bride
Contributor	Mother of the Groom
Contributor	Father of the Groom
Contributor	Bossy Aunt Jeanie
Executor	Disc Jockey
Executor	Florist
Executor	Wedding Officiant
Executor	Caterer
Executory	Wedding Venue Coordinator
Executor	Maid of Honor
Executor	Best Man

What I particularly appreciate about the wedding example is how it highlights the dynamic between the approver and a highly influential contributor. In this scenario, the bride is the decision-maker. However, if the bride's father is funding the wedding, it adds complexity, as he wields some decision-making power. For instance, he could refuse to pay for an expensive disc jockey, effectively holding "pocket veto" authority over decisions.

In summary, regardless of the approach you choose to define your team and decision-making model, it is crucial to invest time upfront in clarifying roles and responsibilities. Doing so establishes basic expectations and ensures you have the necessary resources to deliver the work successfully.

Status Reporting: Avoiding Surprises

Let's face it—people hate surprises. Consider the example of a surprise birthday party. Regardless of the outcome, there are limited scenarios, and all of them have their drawbacks:

1. Scenario One: The party occurs, friends arrive, and the birthday guest appears pleasantly shocked. However, in the back of their mind, they may wonder, "Why did everyone deceive me?" or "Do my friends deceive me often?" These concerns are usually alleviated by the understanding that the party was planned with positive intent.
2. Scenario Two: The birthday guest knows about the event in advance and becomes angry for not having a say in "their" party. Furthermore, they have to fake their surprise during the event.
3. Scenario Three: The event is a total surprise but not the type of celebration they desired. In addition to faking a happy surprise, they also resent not being able to spend their birthday as they had hoped.

This example clearly demonstrates that if surprises are problematic for something as simple as a birthday party, they become exponentially worse in the context of projects. This point is so crucial that I always emphasize my most important expectation when starting a relationship with a new team member or direct report: "I don't like surprises." Whether it's good news or bad news, I want to know as soon as possible.

One of the most effective ways to prevent surprises during a project is by providing regular status updates. Status updates can take various formats, such as standard reports, standing meetings for Agile teams, or project web portals where summary details are maintained. Regardless of the communication method, a status update should include some core elements, as highlighted in the example on the next page.

Project Status Tracking Template		
Project Name:		**Date:**
Overall Status:	**On Track / Off Track**	
Delivery Quality:	**Budget**	**Time**
Launch Quality:	**Outcome Indicator**	
Summary Statement:		
Deliverables Last Week: • • • **Deliverables Next Week:** • • • **Issues / Risks:** • • • **Assistance Needed / Change Requests:** • • •		

The key components of a status report include:

1. **Overall Status:** A visual indicator that quickly communicates whether the project is on track or off track. I personally prefer a binary signal, where only green (on track) or red (at risk) are used. This prevents ambiguity and ensures clarity.

2. **Delivery Quality:** Summary-level indicators of budget, time, percentage of scope delivered, and other relevant resources.

3. **Launch Quality:** One of the most important yet often overlooked indicators. It assesses the probability of achieving the project's intended outcome. Projects should include ongoing research or validation activities to continuously assess launch quality throughout the project's duration.

4. **Summary Statement:** An opportunity for the project manager to share their perspective on the project's progress, trends, and any other relevant information.

5. **Deliverables:** Highlight critical accomplishments and upcoming planned milestones, enabling stakeholders to quickly grasp the work in progress.

6. **Issues & Risks:** A section to highlight problems and potential issues, along with any mitigating factors to avoid surprises.

7. **Assistance & Changes:** If the project team requires assistance or if there are changes in scope that necessitate action from sponsors, it should be clearly communicated.

The example provided serves as a starting point, and organizations can determine the specific information that is most important to them. Different methodologies may require the inclusion of additional status indicators. However, regardless of the format or communication channel used, the primary function of a status report is to prevent surprises. Clear and continuous communication from the project manager, containing information about the project's past, present, and future performance, is essential.

Project Planning Simplified

I once found myself in a discussion with a program manager who took great pride in his talents. He boasted about organizing a highly complex project using a detailed work breakdown structure (WBS) or plan consisting of over 5000 lines. This plan was then translated into sophisticated project planning software, requiring a full-time project coordinator to manage daily plan changes. Intrigued, I asked him, "Do you believe this plan is effective? Are all team members actively engaged in the right tasks at the right time to ensure successful project delivery?" His confidence wavered, and after some defensive statements, he confessed his uncertainty. It wasn't long after that the management team decided to find his replacement.

Oddly enough, this situation reminds me of a scene from a late 1960s war movie called "The Dirty Dozen." The story revolves around a United States military officer chosen to lead a secret mission behind enemy lines during World War II. His team consisted of 12 convicted criminals from the US Army. In one particular scene, the military officer reviews an intricately detailed attack plan with the soldiers, or in this case, the criminals. Surprisingly, the plan is composed of just two elements: a rough map of the target area and a nursery rhyme that outlines the step-by-step activities of their mission. The men repeat the rhyme repeatedly until it is ingrained in their memory. Through this simplicity, each person knew precisely what they needed to do, when they needed to do it, and how their role interconnected with others on the team. In the end, they successfully completed their mission, even without a written plan.

These two stories serve to highlight a crucial point: project plans do not require sophistication to succeed. On the contrary, the best strategies are often simple and easily understandable. At its core, a good project plan serves as a communication tool for team members and stakeholders. In most cases, plans need to outline four essential items:

1. **Description** of the work to be done.
2. **Duration** of each task.
3. **Sequence** of tasks.
4. **Resource requirements** for each task.

To demonstrate how these elements come together, here's an example of a basic project plan for preparing a meal at a fast-food restaurant.

A Five-Minute Project Plan – Preparing a Fast-Food Order					
			Time in minutes and seconds		
Task	Description	Owner	Start	Finish	Duration
1	Place Order for Value Meal	Customer	0:00	0:45	0:45
2	Enter Order in Register	Cashier	0:45	1:15	0:30
3	Collect Payment & Finalize	Cashier	1:15	1:45	0:30
4	Prepare Burger	Burger Chef	1:45	3:45	2:00
5	Prepare Fries	Fry Chef	1:45	2:45	1:00
6	Prepare Drink	Runner	1:45	2:30	0:45
7	Assemble Order	Runner	3:45	4:15	0:30
8	Quality Check	Cashier	4:15	4:30	0:15
9	Call Customer	Cashier	4:30	4:45	0:15
10	Pickup Order	Customer	4:45	5:00	0:15

This plan encompasses all the necessary elements to organize and communicate the work effectively to the team. Each individual knows their assigned task, its start and end times, and the overall flow of activities. Moreover, with a basic plan in place, more sophisticated information can be derived to guide the broader organization. For instance:

- Based on the start and finish times, we can determine that the project will take approximately 5 minutes to complete.

- Apart from the customer, four different team members are required for the work.
- While burger, fries, and drink preparation can occur simultaneously, burger preparation holds critical importance as task #7, assembling the order, cannot begin until the burger is ready. Thus, reducing Burger Preparation time would decrease the overall project duration, unlike reducing Drink Preparation time, which would still result in a 5-minute project.
- Estimation of staffing resources is possible. We know that the cashier requires 1:30, the burger chef requires 2:00, the fry chef requires 1:00, and the runner requires 1:15.
- Project costs can be estimated by aggregating material costs from each task, staffing costs, and potential overhead or contingency allocations.
- These cost estimates can then be compared against the sales price or benefits derived from producing the value meal, providing valuable insights into the project's value potential.
- Identification and mitigation of process risks become feasible. For example, if task owners like the cashier or burger chef fall behind due to allocation on other tasks, the project will face delays. Mitigating actions may involve cross-training staff, such as the runner or fry chef, to perform those tasks.

This example clearly illustrates that a simple project plan serves two crucial purposes:

1. It effectively communicates how the work should be performed, enabling the team to execute it properly.
2. It provides decision-makers with insights to organize individual projects and understand their potential impact on the broader organization.

One of the most common challenges in creating a plan is the

potential for individuals to become overwhelmed by excessive detail, similar to the dispositioned project manager circulating his 5000-line plan. This issue becomes even more pronounced when you're planning complex tasks beyond the scope of making a burger, fries, and a drink. In such cases, I recommend "leveling up" the plan by defining critical milestones within it. These milestones serve as high-level placeholders, under which additional details and tasks can be nested. Let's revisit the project plan for the value meal to demonstrate what this approach looks like:

1. Take Order
2. Prepare Food
3. Deliver Order

Furthermore, for larger projects, it may not be possible to outline detailed tasks beyond a 30- or 60-day timeframe due to incomplete information. In such instances, milestones can serve as suitable placeholders, allowing for resource estimation when detailed information is lacking.

By simplifying project planning and focusing on the essential elements, teams can effectively communicate, execute tasks, and make informed decisions. Keep in mind that complexity does not guarantee success. On the contrary, a clear and concise plan is what empowers teams to achieve their goals efficiently.

Managing Project Budgets

I once had the invaluable experience of serving on a portfolio review board responsible for overseeing numerous projects. One member of the board, a remarkable Senior Vice President, always astounded me with his uncanny ability to instantly spot budget issues in any project. Whenever he raised concerns about a budget, a thorough examination would inevitably reveal significant flaws. Intrigued by his seemingly magical talent, I resolved to uncover his secret. After observing him closely without identifying a pattern, I finally approached him to inquire. Here is how he explained his approach.

"Identifying budget issues is a straightforward task. I swiftly scan the numbers in the budget, focusing on one crucial aspect. I look for any inconsistencies or discrepancies. A well-constructed budget should align seamlessly, with numbers on one document corresponding to those on another. Subtle flaws often emerge in staffing, which I address by referring to standard hourly costs and conducting quick calculations. For example, if a three-month project requires $200,000 in staffing, and the average hourly rate is $50, I question whether 4000 hours of highly skilled labor are truly necessary for the job. Once I spot a flaw, I unravel it like pulling on a thread, knowing that it will likely cause the entire budget to unravel. This enables us to swiftly identify and address the issues, ensuring the budget is reconstructed correctly."

What I found most valuable was that his approach worked in two directions. It not only assisted in identifying issues in other people's projects but also proved exceptionally helpful when crafting a budget for your own project. **Your budget should weave a compelling narrative that can be understood using simple calculations**. That's where I always advise people to begin.

The story conveyed by your project budget should align with your project plan. At a minimum, the plan will help you determine the costs associated with the people and materials required for each task or deliverable.

When referencing your project plan, it's essential to consider that most project costs typically fall into the following categories:

1. **People Costs:** This encompasses the expenses related to the team members performing the work.
2. **Material Costs:** This covers the expenses for any goods needed to complete the project.
3. **Overhead:** This includes costs associated with project management, administration, and other relevant cost allocations, such as office space.
4. **Contingency:** Almost all projects encounter unforeseen issues. It is prudent to allocate a contingency fund to address these challenges.
5. **Ongoing Costs:** While a project has a defined start and end, it may result in deliverables that generate ongoing costs for the organization. Although not necessarily part of the project itself, project managers must define how the effort might impact the entity in perpetuity. This is crucial for assessing the overall benefits.

With an understanding of the common cost categories and a project plan to reference, you can adopt one of two approaches to create your budget:

1. **Bottoms-Up or Zero-Based Budgets:** As the names suggest, you start from scratch and systematically add up various costs, sometimes stratified over time and spend types, to determine the overall budget.
2. **Historical Budgets:** If historical information or examples of budgets from similar projects are available, it is beneficial to leverage them as a reference point for your project.

Personally, I prefer combining these two approaches. An example of a simple project budget summary for a three-phased project is highlighted below.

Project Budget Summary Example				
	Project Phase			
Spend Category	**1**	**2**	**3**	**Total**
Staffing	$100	$500	$200	$800
Materials	$250	$100	-	$350
Overhead	$50	$75	$50	$175
Sub-Total	$400	$675	$250	$1325
Contingency – 15%	$60	$101	$38	$199
Total by Phase	**$460**	**$776**	**$288**	**$1524**

Remember that budgets, much like the plans they are associated with, are never flawless. For larger projects, it is crucial to implement controls to prevent costs from spiraling out of control.

There are two simple actions you can take:

1. Implement a **change control process** within the organization. This means that any scope changes with a significant impact on the project require formal approval and must be reflected in the budget. For instance, if a project involves building a house and a new room is added to the plan, it needs to be approved and accounted for in the budget. Change control and decision-making processes are typically part of team organization.
2. **Release funds incrementally** instead of all at once. I refer to this as the "payroll rule." Just as employees do not receive a year's worth of salary upfront, funding for projects should

be disbursed periodically, linked to project reviews between phases. This mitigates the risk of overspending and allows for timely issue detection and resolution.

By adhering to these principles and adopting a meticulous approach to project budgeting, you can navigate potential budgetary challenges with confidence and keep your project's financial aspects on track.

Communication Plans

In one of my first jobs out of college, I had the opportunity to work in a shampoo factory that also produced mouthwash. This amusingly led to a running joke among employees, as we appreciated the benefits of working alongside colleagues with clean hair and fresh breath. Aside from gaining a newfound respect for personal hygiene, I acquired two key insights during my time there:

1. Most shampoos share common characteristics. Approximately 95% of the product consists of water and a detergent such as sodium lauryl sulfate. It is the remaining 5% of ingredients that set each product apart.

2. Instructions typically advise users to "rinse and repeat."

These two insights offer valuable guidance for communication planning. Whether you are responsible for a global marketing campaign or organizing a grade school bake sale, approximately 95% of the activities involved in developing your communication plan remain the same. The only variations lie in budget and scale. Furthermore, a crucial element for a successful strategy is to repeatedly reinforce primary messages, akin to the concept of rinsing and repeating.

Despite this, I have observed that many projects fail to allocate adequate time and attention to communication planning. Often, individuals become inwardly focused on timelines, budgets, and scope, inadvertently neglecting one of the most important aspects—communicating with those affected by the project.

Communication plans need not be elaborate or complex. In fact, a simple and well-executed plan will invariably yield favorable results.

A straightforward communication planning template that I employ for all my projects is on the next page.

Communication Planning Template			
Why do you need to communicate?			
Who are the core audiences?			
How will you measure success?			
What are your key messages and call to action?			
Who	**What**	**Comm Channel**	**When**

As basic as it may sound, an effective communication plan should always begin by defining the "**why**" of your communication efforts. Too often, people rush to create specific executions such as posters or emails without undertaking the necessary strategic groundwork. It is crucial to invest some upfront time to clarify precisely what you aim to achieve with your communications. This should include defining the strategic objective or intent from the communicator's perspective, rather than solely considering the audience. Using the bake sale example, this could be as simple as "We aim to raise $1000 for our school booster club by selling cookies and brownies."

Once the purpose of your communication is clear, you should

dedicate time to identify the **core audiences** with whom you need to engage to accomplish your objective. A useful approach is to ask yourself, "Who needs to be informed or take action to achieve my strategic objective?" Further clarification can be achieved by exploring questions such as "Are there any specific characteristics about this group?" and "Why would they care about what I have to communicate?"

The next step involves identifying **measures** that will indicate the level of success. These measures can include factors such as adoption, unit sales, dollar sales, views, clicks, sentiment, or any other relevant indicators that help assess the overall effectiveness of your plan.

Now, it is essential to put yourself in the mindset of your audience. Define **key messages** that will be significant and relevant to them. These messages should establish consistent themes to be incorporated into all your communications. Building on the bake sale example, some messages could be "Help support your school by attending our bake sale on Monday" or "Indulge yourself during our Monday bake sale and take a break."

Once you have defined the why, who, how, and what of your communication—i.e., the purpose, audience, success metrics, and key themes—you have established a solid strategic foundation to **develop an executional plan**. The plan itself does not need to be elaborate; a simple outline of each communication, specifying the target audience, message or call to action, communication channel (e.g., email, print, meeting, social media), and frequency, will suffice. Continuously cross-reference each communication against the defined key messages to ensure consistency.

That's it. A fundamental plan grounded in sound principles will consistently yield better results than a disjointed array of executions. And returning to our "rinse and repeat" lesson on shampooing, remember it’s best to overcommunicate your messages.

Risk and Issue Management

I remember reading an article about Lloyds of London issuing an insurance policy for the Rolling Stones guitarist Keith Richards' hands. It was quite amusing to imagine an actuary in London starting his day, reading the news, having a cup of coffee, bidding farewell to his wife, commuting to work on the train, and settling into a cubicle under the glow of fluorescent lights. Then, along comes the boss with some small talk, followed by a casual request to calculate the probability of Keith Richards injuring his hands, so they can draft an insurance policy. Just think about the immense creativity required to consider all the potential scenarios that could lead to Keith Richards injuring his hands. Contrary to popular belief about the insurance industry, I am convinced that actuaries must be some of the most imaginative individuals on the planet.

Fortunately, managing project risks is far simpler than calculating the likelihood of Keith Richards injuring his hands. However, similar to an actuary, it does require a certain level of imagination to contemplate what could go wrong. The project manager's responsibility is to help identify risks, communicate them to stakeholders, devise strategies to minimize the likelihood of their occurrence, and develop contingency plans in case they do materialize.

It is also important to distinguish between risks and issues. A risk is something that has the potential to become an issue, whereas an issue is a risk that has actually manifested. To humorously extend the Keith Richards analogy, a risk might involve his penchant for playing with knives while being drunk, whereas the issue arises if he actually cuts his fingers. To mitigate this risk, you may attempt to restrict his access to knives or alcohol. To address the issue of him actually cutting his fingers, immediate medical attention would be required.

Returning to reality, when it comes to risk management, I find it useful to re-evaluate the project's original premise or purpose. I ask myself, "What factors might diminish the project's benefits or impact its successful completion?"

A good starting point is to assess items related to project delivery since they are often the most straightforward to comprehend. These typically fall within the following risk categories:

- Timeline
- Budget
- Staffing and Resource Availability
- Scope Changes
- Technical Feasibility
- Process Challenges

While delivery-related risks are always a solid starting point, my experience has shown that assumptions regarding benefits represent the most significant risks for most projects. This is because, while a project may encounter changes in time, budget, or scope, it will ultimately fail if the intended benefits are not achieved. Common benefit risk categories to explore include:

- Changes or flawed assumptions concerning **customer insights**
- Shifts in the **competitive environment**
- Evolving trends in **industries or markets**
- Changes in **environmental or socio-political factors**
- Failure to account for **legal or regulatory constraints**

With a basic understanding of common risks, you are now equipped to define and mitigate them. One approach to accomplishing this is by employing "If-Then" statements. For instance, for a given project, you may have a statement such as, "If we do not receive funding by next Friday, then we will be unable to pay our staff, and they will resign." A mitigation strategy for this risk could be something like, "The team will maintain a contingency fund for use in emergencies." This simple format can be translated into a log or tracker that is regularly reviewed with stakeholders.

A basic example of a risk tracker might appear as follows:

Number	Risk	Mitigation
1	**IF** [event] occurs **THEN** this is the impact to the project	Action(s) to minimize risk from becoming an issue
2	**IF** [event] occurs **THEN** this is the impact to the project	Action(s) to minimize risk from becoming an issue
3	**IF** [event] occurs **THEN** this is the impact to the project	Action(s) to minimize risk from becoming an issue

The challenge for the project manager is to help the team differentiate between risks that warrant attention and those that do not. Their role involves maintaining a list of risks and ensuring that appropriate measures are taken to minimize the likelihood of them becoming issues. When executed effectively, your team should be able to avoid potential issues or, at worst, be prepared to respond adeptly if the project veers off track.

If all of this seems a bit overwhelming, remember to inject a bit of fun by employing your imagination. And be grateful that you're not the actuary tasked with devising an insurance policy for a rock 'n roll guitarist.

Waterfall Project Management Methodology

Analogies can be powerful tools for illustrating concepts, and one of my favorite managers had a knack for using them effectively. When discussing the importance of quality, he would often draw a vivid analogy to plane flights. Consider this: in the United States alone, there are over 16 million plane flights per year. Now, imagine if these flights were only 99.5% reliable. The result would be a staggering 220 crashes every single day. Even with a reliability rate of 99.9%, there would still be 44 planes falling out of the sky on a daily basis. This grim image serves as a compelling reminder of the criticality of quality within any process.

Just like air travel, certain projects demand stringent quality control measures, particularly those involving large-scale, highly dependent, or regulated systems. For instance, in the realm of financial services, making iterative changes to core systems that handle banking or sensitive customer information is simply not an option. Even an error affecting a mere 0.001% of people could have severe legal and financial consequences for the business. Consider the implications of a small programming error that alters someone's bank account balance by three or four digits. To avoid such errors, it becomes imperative to design and test system changes meticulously, ensuring a 100% error-free outcome. The complexity and risk level of the system determine the level of rigor applied to testing. This approach is commonly referred to as waterfall, as the project progresses linearly from one phase to the next, with continuous validation. The visual on the next page provides a general representation of a waterfall framework.

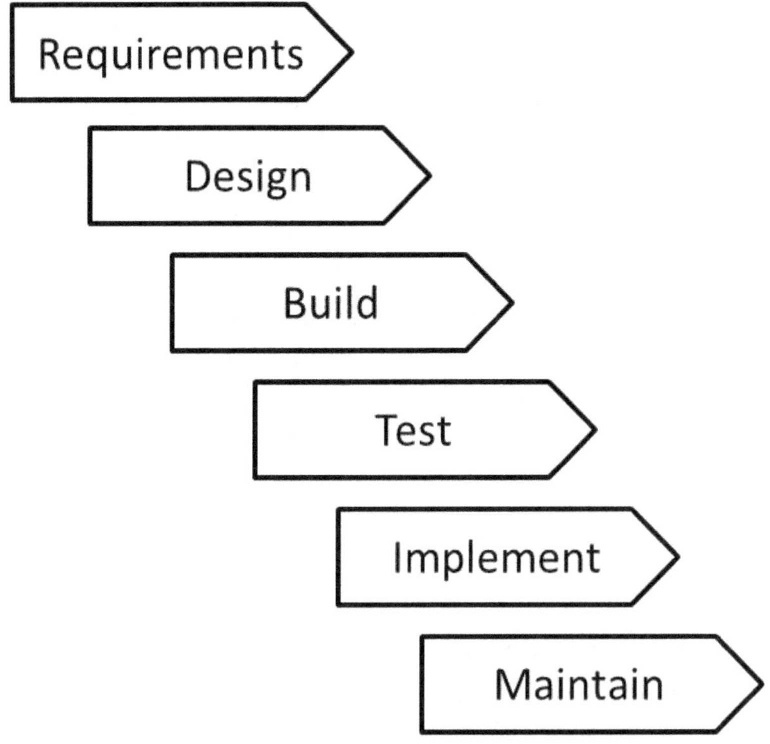

Early in my career as an IT professional, I had the opportunity to work on my first waterfall project, which involved a large-scale enterprise resource planning (ERP) system. My role primarily revolved around configuring, coding, and testing a specific portion of the system. As a relative newcomer to systems development, I was fascinated by the rigorous testing procedures required before implementing any changes. Given that the operations at stake involved potential million-dollar losses per hour, there was absolutely no room for failure. The project followed a traditional waterfall methodology overseen by a multi-functional leadership team. Each step of the process required their "Go-No-Go" decision before progressing further. From my perspective as a developer, the process unfolded as follows:

1. **Requirements gathering:** A business partner would articulate their system needs and provide justifications. An

analyst would capture this information and outline specific requirements. The leadership team would prioritize changes and group them into a release bundle.

2. **Design:** My responsibility was to take the analyst's details and translate them into system design specifications for my designated part. This allowed me to determine the actual scope of configuration and coding required to implement the change. While I focused on my part, coordination was necessary among other team members responsible for different parts of the system. We would meet to review how our designs would work together.

3. **Build:** After documenting the design, we would proceed to "build" or change the system. However, it's important to note that these changes were not made directly in the production system. Instead, we started in a "sandbox" environment—a safe space for exploring configuration and coding without causing disruptions in the business. The sandbox served as a standalone system that simulated production, allowing developers to safely test their updates. Once the changes were understood, they could be replicated in other testing environments for additional validation.

4. **Test:** This phase involved the majority of the time and work. Multiple non-production systems were utilized for testing, based on copies of the production systems to ensure test integrity. The testing steps included:

    - **Unit Testing:** After exiting the sandbox, we developed and tested the updates in individual parts (units) of the system. Various scenarios were explored to ensure the changes performed as expected.

    - **Integration Testing:** Once changes were validated individually, we tested workflows across multiple units. Countless scenarios were examined, deliberately attempting work process errors to ensure no critical data or system integrity failures occurred.

- **User Acceptance Testing:** After technical teams confirmed the functionality of the changes, experienced end users were given access to a test system. This usually included the business partners who initially requested the changes. Similar to integration testing, they conducted numerous end-to-end process tests to validate that the system and changes were behaving as expected. They purposely tried to "break" the system by making errors and also assessed the benefits of the changes for the organization based on their daily work.

- **Stress Testing:** In addition to testing work processes, it was crucial to understand how the changes might impact overall system performance. Stress testing involved automating workflows with high throughput levels to identify potential breakdown points and inefficient processes that could slow down the system. Detected issues were addressed and reworked as necessary.

- **Cut Over Testing:** This was the final test, simulating the implementation of changes in the production system. Unforeseen issues could arise during this transition, especially concerning the integrity of databases, interdependent systems, and active workflows. Cut over testing served as the last practice run before moving the release to production. Technical teams conducted several "simulation" test implementations in a system that mirrored production almost perfectly. The simulation ensured that everyone knew their roles during the actual implementation and helped identify possible risks or issues. At this point, the governance team made the final "Go-No Go" decision to proceed with the release.

5. **Implement:** In parallel with testing, constant communication and training were conducted to prepare end users for the update. Communication efforts peaked during the weeks surrounding the implementation. Personally, the implementation phase evoked a combination of excitement and anticipation, as my work would finally be moved into a "real" production system. While waiting for any potential issues to arise, I would utilize my time to prepare for future projects and change requests.

6. **Maintain:** This marked the transition of full responsibility to subject matter experts and technical support, who would maintain the system and assist end users with ongoing questions or issues. In essence, the maintenance phase signaled the end of the project, as the organization and system resumed normal operations.

This example of my own experience demonstrates how a waterfall project is executed from one person's point of view. The most important takeaway is the extreme importance of quality control and testing when dealing with high-risk systems. There are more detailed references available that provide specific guidance for waterfall projects. If you are new to these types of projects, I recommend reviewing resources from ITIL (Information Technology Infrastructure Library) as a starting point.

Agile Project Management Methodology

One of the remarkable aspects of agile is that it has a manifesto. I mean, how many other project management methodologies can boast having a manifesto? What's even more fascinating is that this manifesto was written at a ski resort in Snowbird, Utah. I'm an avid skier and must confess that after a day on the slopes the last thing you would find me doing is producing a manifesto about project management methodologies. But, let's not digress. Before delving into agile, it is best to begin by sharing the actual manifesto:

Manifesto for Agile Software Development

We are uncovering better ways of developing software by doing it and helping others do it. Through this work, we have come to value:

- Individuals and interactions over processes and tools
- Working software over comprehensive documentation
- Customer collaboration over contract negotiation
- Responding to change over following a plan

That is, while there is value in the items on the right, we value the items on the left more.

Signed by: Kent Beck, Mike Beedle, Arie van Bennekum, Alistair Cockburn, Ward Cunningham, Martin Fowler, James Grenning, Jim Highsmith, Andrew Hunt, Ron Jeffries, Jon Kern, Brian Marick, Robert C. Martin, Steve Mellor, Ken Schwaber, Jeff Sutherland, Dave Thomas

From the manifesto, I have identified two primary takeaways:

1. Agile is primarily designed for **software development**. In other words, agile is not intended to guide the creation of FDA regulated drugs, airplanes, or large buildings.
2. Agile is **more about culture than process**. It embraces an action-oriented spirit that encourages us to stop over-analyzing and start doing meaningful work that people need right now.

However, agile did not emerge spontaneously as a methodology. It has been built on the insights of numerous individuals who have applied various approaches such as Scrum, iterative methods, Kanban, Theory of Constraints (TOC), and more to tackle challenging problems. Consequently, just like other movements that begin with manifestos, there exist countless interpretations of what agile truly is and how it should be used.

Personally, I have employed agile approaches on numerous projects, and the results have been exceptional. Like any tool, agile must be matched with the appropriate situation. Just as a hammer cannot properly insert a screw, agile is only effective when applied to the right type of work. For instance, during my time as a partner at a small marketing consultancy, we successfully utilized agile to manage all our website and e-commerce projects. Agile enabled us to quickly deliver a minimum viable product (MVP), gather feedback, adapt to changes in scope, and ultimately deliver solutions that delighted our clients. A visual outlining our approach is highlighted on the next page:

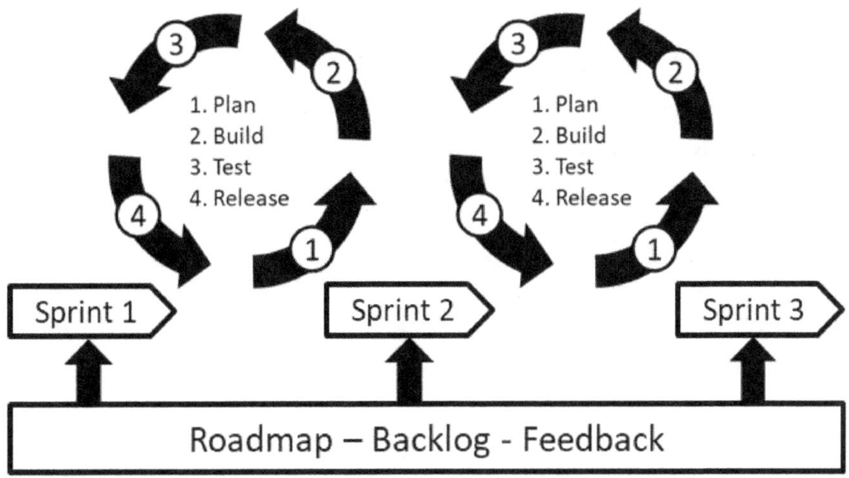

Firstly, we would engage with our customers to discuss their needs. We explored their website usage, target audience, preferred layouts, core functionality, and more. Subsequently, we would outline a one-page product roadmap that highlighted the MVP and planned releases of additional functionality. Once aligned, we would embark on our first sprint to develop the most basic website possible. Our sprints typically lasted a week and consisted of a simple work plan, development and testing, and a production release. Development occupied the majority of our time. After each release, I would gather feedback from our customers, update the backlog with any necessary changes or fixes, and make adjustments to the roadmap when needed. This informed the priorities for upcoming sprints. We continued this iterative process until the work was completed and the customer was satisfied.

Agile can be adapted to various situations, with the timeframe being the most common variation. For example, some dedicated product teams may conduct daily sprints instead of weekly ones. These daily sprints often involve a collaborative "stand-up" meeting, where the team reviews customer feedback, reprioritizes the backlog, and updates the roadmap or plan.

As previously mentioned, agile represents a cultural shift. Whether the team meets daily or weekly, the work is always customer-centric, adaptable to change, and action-oriented. Moreover, practicing agile does not necessarily require extensive training or specialized certifications. With the manifesto and an agile framework at hand, most competent teams are capable of self-organizing.

SECTION 2

The Art of Project Management

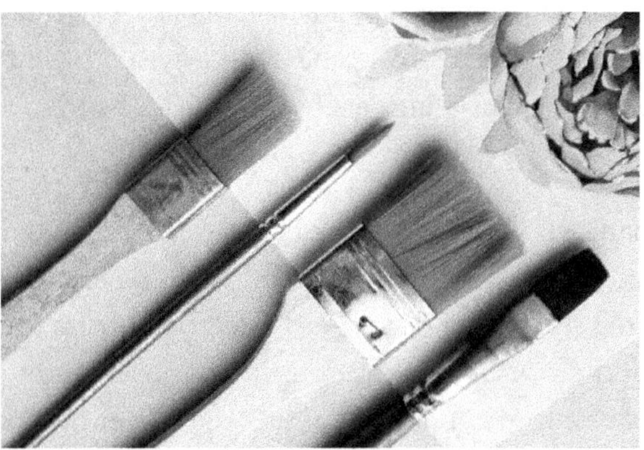

Projects necessitate effective organization of people, who are inherently diverse, possessing different wants, needs, and perspectives. To excel as a project manager, it is crucial to establish connections with people and embody a confident leadership style. Despite the implications of the term "art," creativity is not a prerequisite. Rather, it requires practice and a willingness to allow your personal style to naturally emerge. In this section we will explore various techniques, stories, and approaches designed to help you discover and develop your own unique leadership capabilities.

[Image by Martina Bulková from Pixabay]

Project Management Wisdom from a Samurai

I found myself revisiting "The Book of Five Rings," written by Miyamoto Musashi, a renowned samurai from the 17th century. Musashi was not only an undefeated swordsman in over 60 duels to the death but was also an accomplished artist and writer. His philosophy transcends battle strategies and sword fighting, offering profound insights applicable to skilled project management. I believe there is one quote from Musashi's writings that captures the essence of what sets a competent project manager apart. The translation goes as follows: "Perception is strong and sight is weak. In strategy, it is important to see distant things as if they are close and to take a distanced view of close things."

A project manager is uniquely positioned to strike a balance between the macro and micro perspectives of work. While executives or sponsors often maintain a distant view, removed from the daily intricacies of the work, and project team members tend to focus on the immediate tasks without considering the bigger picture, the project manager sees both.

Based on Musashi's wisdom, I propose three guidelines for project managers to follow:

1. **Maintain a Strategic Focus:** While managing a project, avoid becoming overly absorbed in the day-to-day details of each individual task. It is essential to remain aware of how well you are progressing towards the overall goal. Failing to do so can lead the team astray without even realizing it. The proverbial death by a thousand paper cuts.

2. **Consider the Broader Implications:** When confronted with small tactical changes, take a moment to reflect on how they might impact the larger project, company, or organization. Known as the "butterfly effect," a minor event can potentially alter the outcome of an entire plan.

3. **Monitor the External Environment:** Be vigilant about changes in the external landscape that could significantly impact your current situation. Look beyond the immediate vicinity of your project and stay informed about shifting organizational priorities, industry trends, competition, and relevant social, political, and economic developments.

In addition to these guidelines, incorporating practical tools and approaches can enhance your work as a project manager. Here are a few suggestions, presented in no particular order:

- **Create a Roadmap:** Develop a high-level, time-based visual representation of your project or portfolio. Put it on one page. This could be a simple Gantt chart or a multi-year portfolio visualization. Regularly review the roadmap to identify opportunities and potential risks.
- **Engage with External Stakeholders:** Set aside time to connect with individuals outside your project, organization, or company. This could involve having coffee or lunch with them or attending informational meetings. By doing so, you can stay attuned to political or organizational dynamics that may impact your team.
- **Stay Informed of the External Landscape:** Dedicate 10 to 15 minutes of your day to read news relevant to your industry, competition, or related social, political, and economic environments. This habit will ensure you are aware of trends or activities that could have implications for your work.

While these tools and approaches are not exhaustive, they provide a solid starting point for continuous improvement. And if, for any reason, the musings of a 17th-century samurai may not seem directly relevant in today's world, let me leave you with one final quote from Musashi, in the hopes that it may inspire you in your daily quest for personal and professional growth: "Today is victory over yourself of yesterday, so tomorrow you will be victorious over lesser men."

Getting People to Show Up on Your Project

I've always enjoyed the self-deprecating humor of Woody Allen. One of his attributed quotes goes something like this: "80% of success in life is showing up," with various additions such as "and the other 20% is luck." Good comedy often carries a kernel of truth in its punchline, and I've come to realize that Woody Allen was right. Reflecting on the projects I've witnessed fail versus those that have succeeded, a major contributing factor to success is getting the right people to show up. Although it may sound incredibly simple, it is, in fact, a challenging task.

Whenever I embark on a project or encounter one that is not progressing well, I consistently ask myself, "Am I getting the right people to show up?" This encompasses sponsors, stakeholders, and individuals specialized in performing specific tasks, among others. Due to the dynamic nature of projects, this is a question that a competent project manager should continually revisit.

Fortunately, there exists a variety of proven project management tools and tactics that can be employed. Here are some examples:

- **Project Charter:** In addition to formalizing the scope of work, a project charter should outline the team members responsible for project delivery.
- **Formal Kick-Off:** When initiating a project, a kick-off meeting brings together all the stakeholders to provide visibility and acts as an invitation for ongoing participation.
- **Project Roles and Responsibilities:** In larger endeavors, it is advisable to formalize the definitions of individual roles and responsibilities within an organizational chart, enabling clear expectations.
- **RASCI or PACE Chart:** These tools complement the organizational chart by clarifying decision-making processes

and identifying key individuals who must show up to execute the work.

- **Meeting Invitations:** While seemingly obvious, when scheduling meetings, it is crucial to continuously review the invitees, ensuring that key stakeholders are included and monitoring the presence of the right people.
- **Capacity Plans:** Typically integrated into portfolio planning, capacity plans can ensure that the necessary individuals are available to show up when required. A basic plan will indicate what percentage of time or total number of hours a person will be dedicated to your project.
- **Offer Free Snacks:** What can I say. People love free food and if they have to choose between two meetings, one with free food and one without, I think we all know which one they'll choose.

While there are no rigid rules, I can confidently say that getting the right people to show up will make or break any project. Countless times, I've witnessed projects veer off course, only to realize that the root cause was a lack of engagement from the right people.

This brings us back to another Woody Allen quote, "Confidence is what you have before you understand the problem." Of course, while it's not quite as funny, I would say that: "Confidence comes from ensuring you have the right people showing up on your project."

Knowing Your Burn and Churn

One of my favorite bands is "They Might Be Giants," and one of my all-time favorite album covers is from their 1980s single entitled "Don't Let's Start." The cover art showcases a picture of a snowman elegantly dressed in a top hat, scarf, and mittens. What makes the image peculiar is that the snowman is warming itself by a large pile of burning money, causing it to melt into a puddle. I still have an old T-shirt in a dresser somewhere with this image on it.

I must admit that I'm not entirely sure why I shared this anecdote, except for the fact that the image from that album cover always comes to mind when discussing "burn rates." In the realm of projects, burn rates refer to the average amount of resources, primarily money, that your project consumes on a regular basis. It represents the constant costs that aid in estimating when your resources might deplete. For instance, if your project has a budget of $120,000 and you're burning an average of $10,000 per month on labor, you will exhaust your funds in 12 months. Think of it as a fire that ceases burning once it has consumed all the available resources.

In contrast, projects also involve "churn," which pertains to the variable costs. For instance, when constructing a house, you may need to make an initial significant payment for lumber, concrete, nails, and so on. These are one-time expenditures and differ from the daily wages you pay to the building crew. As a project manager, it is crucial to plan and prepare for substantial "churn" events to avoid any significant surprises in your budget.

By adopting the habit of assessing both your burn and churn, you can minimize unexpected surprises and potential delays caused by resource scarcity.

Think Like an Owner

Some may perceive me as having an "Ebenezer Scrooge complex." That's because I hate spending money. One aspect of business that captivates me is the ability to measure and quantify success through financial gains. Creating things that generate monetary value provides a tangible sense of accomplishment.

However, it is often overlooked that the owner is the last person in a business to get ever paid. If expenses exceed revenue, the distributions go to everyone else involved. In such instances, the owner may find themselves empty-handed or even in debt. Repeated experiences like this lead owners to view everything through profit and loss-colored lenses, where black and red dominate.

Owners naturally develop a heightened awareness of every cost associated with the business—COGS (cost of goods sold), administrative expenses, labor, rent, taxes, insurance, regulatory fees, legal fees, professional fees, office supplies, marketing expenses, utilities, and even the luxury bottled water in the refrigerator. Nothing escapes their scrutiny.

Yet, it is not solely about costs. It is also about ensuring that every action the business undertakes creates value. It is about enhancing products or services, reaching new customers, and fostering growth.

Seeing the world in black and red allows for a pragmatic spotlight to illuminate every task, cost, or activity. **When this perspective is genuine and well-intentioned, it possesses the potential to surpass any process improvement methodology available.**

Most entrepreneurs are naturally inclined to see the world through this lens. Case in point. I once encountered the founder of a mid-sized company during a marketing proposal meeting. With three members of his leadership team present, he opened the discussion by remarking, "This better be good because this meeting is costing me

$1250." That's right. He was mentally calculating the potential return on investment of our meeting. It was at that moment I knew I had found someone who spoke my language. And indeed, he accepted our proposal.

As businesses grow larger, fewer employees maintain the black and red perspective. This is not their fault; roles become more specialized, individuals become further removed from the product or service, and employees receive their compensation regardless of the owner's situation. Consequently, large groups of seemingly intelligent people find themselves engaged in meetings to plan for other meetings—a reality perfectly captured by the popular comic strip, Dilbert.

The risk of this approach lies in solely viewing the business through the black and red lens, as it can lead to being "a penny wise and pound foolish." There are myriad other perspectives to consider, including those of your customers, employees, competitors, and the broader community in which you operate. A good leader must maintain a holistic perspective across all these dimensions.

Therefore, I recommend that whether you are an owner, a mid-level manager, or even the janitor cleaning the floors, take a day—perhaps once a month—to mentally don your black and red glasses. Shine that pragmatic spotlight and seek opportunities to eliminate unnecessary costs or find new sources of value. Even small improvements can yield significant results.

Let Reality be the Judge

Working as a partner at a small business marketing agency has taught me numerous lessons. One of the most crucial ones is to avoid getting entangled in conflicting opinions. It's easy to become fixated on a particular creative design, marketing tactic, or tagline. This is especially challenging for me because I hold strong viewpoints and relish being "right." I mean, who doesn't?

However, here's what I've discovered: **it's far more important to be "effective" than to be "right."** And here's a secret: being effective is actually much easier than being right!

What I find fascinating about marketing is that you can experiment with multiple approaches simultaneously. If you're torn between two different creative concepts, why not try both? If you have five different advertising headlines, why not test them all? If you believe your message might resonate with a different audience, go ahead and share it with them to see what happens. All you need to do is let reality be the judge. The true measure of what's "right" lies in the actual results. Focus on doing more of what generates the best outcomes and less of what doesn't.

This approach is the essence of modern marketing campaigns. It's called A/B testing, and most organizations use it to continuously optimize and adapt to changing conditions.

The best part is that adopting this mindset isn't limited to marketing. It can be applied to various aspects such as retail design, portfolio management, vendor selection, computer programming, websites, sourcing, startup investing, and even aspects of organizational design.

So, the next time you find yourself becoming hindered by differing opinions, consider exploring ways to test multiple paths simultaneously. While you may not always achieve the satisfaction of being "right," it will significantly enhance overall effectiveness.

Praise Publicly, Criticize Privately

I learned a valuable lesson early in my career as a young manager in my early 20s. I had several direct reports, including a manager in his late 50s whom we'll refer to as Bill to maintain anonymity. Bill brought a wealth of experience and a pragmatic approach to his work. Unfortunately, due to my youthful arrogance, I failed to fully appreciate the expertise he brought to the table, and I made a foolish mistake.

As part of my responsibilities, I oversaw Information Technology capabilities at multiple production facilities, with Bill in charge of IT operations at one of the sites. Regrettably, there were systemic issues impacting the reliability of our technology at his site, which were beyond his control. In an effort to address these concerns, I decided to meet with the plant manager and reassure him of our commitment to resolving the problem.

With little preparation I brought Bill along to the meeting. To my surprise the plant manager was much angrier than I had anticipated. In the heat of the moment, I found myself saying, "Bill could have done a much better job addressing these issues for you. I will personally address this with him after our meeting to ensure it doesn't happen again."

Immediately after the meeting, Bill pulled me aside and, with a serious expression on his face, firmly grabbed my arm, looked me in the eye, and said, "Please don't ever criticize my work in public like that ever again. If you have an issue with my performance, address it with me directly." Initially, I felt the urge to argue since there were real problems with our operations, but I quickly realized he was right. I had committed the rookie manager mistake of publicly criticizing one of my team members. Moreover, I knew that Bill had consistently delivered excellent work. Reflecting on the situation, I understood the implications of my actions:

1. It conveyed to my team member that I was not supportive of him. Said differently, I didn't "have his back."

2. It indicated to the plant manager that I lacked an understanding of the problem and was incapable of managing my own team effectively.

3. As the primary IT leader at the factory, I had also tarnished Bill's reputation with the local plant manager, which may limit his effectiveness in the future.

To this day I am grateful that Bill had the courage to confront me immediately about my mistake. I had learned the lesson of praising people in public and criticizing them in private the hard way. Fortunately, he recognized my lack of experience and forgave me. My hope is that others don't make this same mistake.

Large Projects Require Clear Vision

Sometimes projects can become overwhelming and collapse under their own weight, or they may linger indefinitely like a hurricane offshore that never makes landfall. These situations are disappointing because they hold promise but ultimately result in losses. The primary challenge in managing extraordinarily large projects lies in the immense complexity they entail. However, establishing a shared vision is one element that can help overcome this obstacle. Let me provide an example of how this can be achieved.

I was part of a strategic programs team known for being called in to rescue projects that had veered off track or to accelerate initiatives with high value potential. One of the most challenging projects I encountered was a supply chain transformation. Supply chains are inherently complex, and this particular project presented an opportunity to eliminate waste of hundreds of millions of dollars through improved visibility, control, and automated decision-making. However, it required a solution that touched thousands of physical locations, involved numerous business partners, and incorporated various technologies. Additionally, it spanned over twenty different countries. Initially, the project seemed like an enormous jigsaw puzzle with no clear picture of where the pieces fit.

The jigsaw analogy proved to be apt. After engaging with multiple stakeholders, it became evident that there was no shared vision for what success looked like. Each person had a different perspective on the completed puzzle. Recognizing this lack of alignment and the complexity involved, I realized the necessity of establishing a common and detailed vision.

To achieve this, I organized a one-week working session involving all subject matter experts, systems owners, and business partners. Over 50 people participated in the event. The goal was to create a detailed vision that outlined the necessary processes, systems, and workflows to deliver the desired benefits. The event consisted of iterative daily work sessions, with individual teams focusing on specific aspects of the supply chain and collectively sharing their recommendations to ensure alignment. Some key elements that contributed to the success of the event included:

1. Strong **executive sponsorship** to emphasize support for the project.
2. A rough **outline of the solution** as a starting point for feedback and collaboration.
3. A **diverse group** that included external experts.
4. Small and large group **work sessions** to leverage everyone's expertise.
5. Active **issue tracking** with prompt follow-up.
6. A well-structured **schedule** to keep participants engaged.
7. An **offsite location** to minimize distractions from daily operations.

By the fourth day of the work session, we had developed a detailed vision of the solution. By the fifth day, we had a clear list of next steps to advance the project. Since all key stakeholders contributed to the design, they understood the necessary trade-offs within their respective areas to achieve the common goal. This shared understanding proved critical during later stages of the project, given the uneven distribution of costs and benefits.

Armed with a collective and detailed vision, we were able to move forward with a clear work plan. The project took several years to complete, but we successfully realized the anticipated benefits. While sound project management principles played a crucial role throughout, in hindsight, the detailed vision was one of the primary factors that prevented this massive project from becoming a slow moving hurricane consuming resources across the organization.

The "Broccoli and Sauce" Change Management Technique

I once had the opportunity to facilitate a change management training session for a leadership team. Throughout the training, we delved into various challenges they were encountering. As a "horizontal" team responsible for delivering operational and technology solutions across multiple organizations, they faced a recurring issue that followed a specific pattern:

1. Identification of a significant cost savings opportunity in a process or technology.
2. Documentation and sharing of the opportunity with an executive business sponsor in the affected organization.
3. Funding and prioritization of the work by the sponsor.
4. Successful implementation of the change.
5. Resistance from the end users, who would go to great lengths to express their dissatisfaction with the new solution, even resorting to back channels to complain to the sponsor.

This repetitive scenario had severely undermined the organization's credibility, despite the fact that the solutions they developed were actually effective and brought substantial value to the business.

To address this problem, I shared a relatable story about a mother shopping with her kids at a supermarket. If you've ever experienced shopping with young children, this anecdote will likely resonate with you. Whenever the kids passed by candy or cookies, they would get excited and try to place them in the cart. Occasionally, the mother would allow them to pick one treat, but she would continue shopping for nutritious food for their dinner. When they reached the produce section, the kids would wrinkle their noses and exclaim, "Eewww! Put that back! We don't want broccoli; it tastes yucky!" However, the mother would still buy the broccoli. Later, when dinner time arrived, she would serve the broccoli with a delicious cheese sauce. At that point, the kids would happily eat the broccoli, and everyone was satisfied—they were consuming healthy food that tasted even better.

After sharing a few laughs about our own experiences with getting kids to eat vegetables, I prompted the team to consider which characters they represented in the story. It became evident that they had been identifying themselves as the mother all along, when in reality, the "mom" was the business sponsor. The end users, in this analogy, were the children. With this fresh perspective, it became clear that no matter how effectively they communicated with the end users, it was ultimately the responsibility of the business sponsor to relay the changes to their organization. Just as there comes a time when a mother needs to tell her kids to eat their vegetables, even if they only want dessert, the business sponsor must guide the end users towards embracing the change.

From that day forward, the organization implemented the "Broccoli and Sauce" change management plan for every project. While they continued to communicate changes to the end users, their primary focus shifted to creating communication materials—referred to as the "cheese sauce"—to empower their sponsors. These materials included presentations, draft emails, recorded webinars, and more. They complemented these efforts with a well-structured communication plan organized by the project manager to ensure its execution by the sponsor. This seemingly minor adjustment made a tremendous difference in the success and adoption rates of their projects. It also strengthened their relationship with the sponsor, reducing the impact of back-channel complaints about their work.

Everyday Change Management

Let's face it: most of us are resistant to change. Even the smallest changes can sometimes provoke strong reactions. Menu updates at our favorite restaurant, software updates to our phones, or even rearranging products in our local supermarket can trigger rants. Whether we like it or not, the frequency of change across all aspects of our lives is exponentially increasing. Futurist Ray Kurzweil fittingly described our current era as "The Age of Acceleration."

Constant change places overwhelming demands on daily leadership responsibilities and often leads to frustration and burnout. Yet, once we recognize and accept change as an integral part of everyday life—not just a special activity reserved for HR or project management professionals—we can begin to approach it as a capability that we all need to develop.

Having been deeply involved in significant change management efforts throughout my career, I have observed several practices that consistently yield valuable results. I consider these the five daily practices for change management—approaches that can be utilized by anyone, at any level, to effectively manage the constant stream of change. Whether you are the CEO or an entry-level team member, you have the power to proactively lead positive change each day.

Here are five habits that every leader can employ to manage everyday change:

1. **Look Beyond the Organization**: People often find themselves blindsided by change when they lose touch with the broader world around them. It is crucial to stay informed about market trends, new competitors, and sources of disruption. This can be as simple as staying updated through trade publications, attending conferences, or keeping up with the news. Gain new perspectives by breaking free from your daily routine. For instance, if you work in accounting at a

large corporation, consider taking a "field trip" to learn about the practices of accountants in smaller organizations, and vice versa. Continually explore how new insights can impact your work and actively seek ways to keep yourself and your team relevant.

2. **Stay Connected with the People you Serve:** Disconnection from understanding the ever-changing wants, needs, and expectations of the people you serve can lead to mistakes. Regardless of whether you work in sales, marketing, operations, IT, engineering, accounting, HR, finance, or any other area within the organization, there are individuals who rely on the work you do. Take the time to meet with them, discuss ways to improve, and even explore alternative means for meeting their needs. These interactions can occur formally through scheduled meetings or informally over coffee or lunch.

3. **Measure Outcomes:** Positive change is ultimately about consistently achieving better outcomes. While commercial aspects of the business may have clear outcome metrics such as revenue and profit, tracking results in the back-office may appear more challenging. However, this is not the case. Adoption rates, usage statistics, satisfaction levels, defect rates, costs, process completion times, effort required to complete a process, total outputs, and other similar indicators all provide means to assess outcomes. As long as you can correlate changes with improved outcomes, you can be confident that you are moving in the right direction.

4. **Foster Continuous Communication:** Communication lies at the core of successful change management. Leaders must establish diverse and ongoing communication channels with their stakeholders. These channels should enable open and honest feedback based on mutual trust. Examples include meetings, one-on-one conversations, newsletters, training sessions, videos, chats or forums, intranet sites, emails, or even a traditional bulletin board. Establish a consistent

rhythm of communication and adapt it as the needs of your audience evolve.

5. **Establish a Vision and Edit as Needed:** Managing continuous change does not mean responding to every whim or issue that arises. Instead, leaders must set a clear vision of where they are heading while remaining open to incorporating changes along the way. Begin by developing a roadmap or plan and consider utilizing project management and operational methodologies such as agile and Kanban. This approach will enable you to maintain progress in the right direction while incorporating new information as it becomes available.

By incorporating these five practices into your daily routine, you can effectively navigate the ever-changing landscape and proactively drive positive change. Remember, everyone has the ability to be a leader and make a difference every single day.

Killing Zombie Projects

Zombies captivate audiences on television due to their relentless nature, making them incredibly difficult to eliminate. Surprisingly, the world of "zombie projects" exists in real life as well. If you have worked in a large company, chances are you have encountered at least one of these projects lurking around. These aimless endeavors wander through the organization, devouring valuable resources without producing any meaningful results. It's undeniably terrifying.

To contribute to the prevention of a zombie project apocalypse, I have compiled a comprehensive field guide to aid aspiring zombie hunters. This guide will assist you in identifying and eradicating these dreaded undead projects that may be lurking within your organization.

Let's begin with the basics: classification. Here is a brief overview of the zombie projects you may encounter:

1. *Ploddus Alongus* - The most common type. These projects drag on endlessly without making any tangible progress. As a defense mechanism, they often generate PowerPoint presentations to create an illusion of productivity. However, don't be deceived! Ignoring them won't lead to their demise. They are notorious for draining resources from more important work and should never be overlooked.
2. *Amorphous Resurrectus* - Difficult to detect, these projects typically emerge after a project has been canceled. Like a ghoul rising from the grave, they resurface weeks, months, or even years after the original project's failure. These grotesque abominations retain 95% of the characteristics of the previous project but assume a new identity to evade detection.
3. *Gravitas Blobulous* - Rare, voracious, and extremely dangerous. While its origins are difficult to pinpoint, it is believed to be a severely mutated version of Ploddus Alongus. One leading

> hypothesis suggests that Ploddus Alongus consumes enough resources to reach a critical mass, resulting in the project's excessive gravity, which then draws more resources from its surroundings. One unmistakable sign is the presence of swarms of buzzwords, akin to flies buzzing around a corpse, attempting to defend the project. They entice their prey with the illusion of progress, claiming that "with more assistance, we can make significant headway." However, instead of progress, they devour precious resources, which are never to be seen again.

Now equipped with a general understanding of the various classifications, you are ready to embark on your hunt!

First and foremost, when you encounter a zombie project, identify it as such. This simple yet courageous act can often raise enough awareness to eliminate it. Remember, sunlight is a powerful disinfectant.

However, if despite your efforts to draw attention to a zombie project it persists, more drastic measures are required. You need to quantify the wastage in terms of time, money, and human resources. Push for a thorough evaluation of the project's benefits and prepare a return on investment (ROI) summary that vividly demonstrates the damage being done. Present this compelling offering to a "higher power," someone with the authority to intervene and swiftly put an end to the project.

If all else fails, it's time to become a full-fledged zombie killer! Embrace your inner Bruce Campbell (aka Ash) from Evil Dead. Just as silver bullets are effective against werewolves and wooden stakes against vampires, you must destroy the zombie project's brain to truly eliminate it. Admittedly, this is no easy task!

Successfully eliminating the most relentless undead projects requires a skillful combination of techniques. Since each situation is unique, it falls upon you to determine the most suitable approach. Here are some strategies to add to your arsenal:

- **Constant Sunlight:** Utilize every opportunity to shed light on the project. Remember, sometimes it takes multiple doses of a medicine to completely eradicate a disease.
- **Amputation of Non-Infected Parts:** Identify the healthy aspects of the project that might still be salvageable and separate them to develop independently. This approach exposes the core problem areas and limits excuses to keep the project alive.
- **Focus on the Light:** Sometimes individuals support zombie projects because they believe there are no alternatives. Help them "see the light" by sharing examples of more valuable activities they could pursue instead.
- **Logic:** Zombie projects often thrive on emotions, which serve as a major source of their power. Apply logic to the situation and encourage others to do the same. Recognizing and reducing emotional attachment is an effective way to facilitate a peaceful "letting go" of the project, allowing it to die.
- **Invoke Multiple "Higher Powers":** Share your ROI summary with multiple decision-makers. Occasionally, a collective effort is required to vanquish an exceptionally resilient monster.
- **Starvation:** Deprive the project of talent and funding. This can slow down its progress and potentially bring it to a complete halt.

A final word of caution: Zombie projects can draw power from dark allies. These may include external consultants, outside vendors, naive co-workers, and sponsors who are directly influenced by the project. Before attempting to eliminate a zombie project, ensure you understand the true extent of its power base. Just like removing weeds, effective extermination requires uprooting all the roots.

There you have it. Equipped with this knowledge, you are prepared to confront the persistent undead projects that plague your workplace. With practice and a touch of good fortune, you can contribute to making the world a better place!

Start Backwards to Go Forward

Earlier in my career as a project manager, I was faced an Olympic-sized challenge. What initially began as an idea to have a few brands advertise during the Winter Olympic games swiftly evolved into a complex program involving over 10 different brand teams, numerous creative agencies, various retail promotions, and a significant on-ground presence at the games themselves. However, it was more than just a marketing endeavor; it became an authentic tribute to world-class athletes and the sacrifices made by their families. The stakes were high, and we had to deliver flawlessly.

In a surreal moment, I found myself sitting on a small leadership team with the Chief Marketing Officer. He outlined our task: executing one of the largest marketing campaigns in the company's history within a mere four months. He placed his trust in us to achieve excellence.

For project managers, challenges like these are dreams come true, and I am forever grateful for the opportunity. Throughout this endeavor, one of the most effective project planning techniques we employed was visualizing a successful outcome. Consistent with the Olympic theme, it's worth noting that high-performing athletes also rely on this technique.

Despite the urgency surrounding us, we resisted the temptation to dive headfirst into the detailed work. Instead, we took a brief time-out to define the minimum scope. Given that the games spanned over two weeks, we meticulously outlined every single activity and marketing deliverable or event on the calendar. We visualized this information on large-scale posters, distributing them to every supporting team. Through this process, we were able to work backwards to identify redundancies and unnecessary deliverables. Once alignment was achieved, the posters served as a guiding light, ensuring everyone's actions were aligned with our vision. Subsequently, we developed the cross functional project plans by working backward to determine the essential activities that "must be true" in order to deliver each individual execution.

This approach allowed us to clearly communicate our vision for success, swiftly address any issues impeding progress, and focus our efforts on the most critical tasks. Additionally, it empowered us to eliminate or disregard any scope that did not contribute value. Granted, not everything went perfectly, but in the end, we achieved our goal.

If you ever find yourself overwhelmed by the sheer magnitude or compressed timeframe of a project, here's a suggestion: avoid the temptation to immediately start executing. Instead, invest in visualizing the desired outcome, eliminate the unnecessary, and craft your plan by working backward. By aligning everyone with a shared vision, you will establish a solid foundation for successful project management.

Project Management vs. Project Leadership

One of the most pivotal moments in my career took place during my tenure as an assistant brand manager. I was entrusted with the task of leading a strategic project aimed at analyzing our product portfolio and devising recommendations to streamline our overall product mix. Driven by a desire to excel, I meticulously scrutinized historical sales data from every conceivable angle. After weeks of effort, I finally presented my findings to the marketing director. However, my moment of horror occurred a mere 45 seconds into my presentation. The director turned to my manager and posed the direct question, "What are we really going to do?" Without skipping a beat, my manager promptly offered an alternative strategy that proved to be robust and foolproof.

This experience stands out as one of the most enlightening moments of my professional journey. Even to this day, I remain indebted to my manager for affording me the opportunity to stumble and, simultaneously, demonstrating what it means to exhibit strategic leadership.

Allow me to explain where I went awry. My entire analysis was based on highlighting the products that, when removed, would result in the least reduction in sales. Yes, you read that correctly - my recommendation essentially revolved around the idea that reducing products would diminish sales. In no uncertain terms, it was a bad idea.

As foolish as my recommendation was, it dawned on me that when faced with formidable challenges, many of us tend to gravitate towards minimizing losses. It provides a sense of security, serves as a defensive measure in the face of potential failure, and is a horrible way to run a business!

In stark contrast, the strategy put forth by my manager sought to leverage the change as an opportunity for business growth. Reducing products became a catalyst for increasing sales! He outlined how eliminating certain products would enable us to simplify our offerings, reduce complexity and costs for our retail partners, generate excitement to secure new points of distribution, and strategically refocus our advertising efforts to support our higher-margin products. This approach was eventually implemented, resulting in significant business expansion.

The profound lesson I learned during that period has resonated with me throughout my entire career. **Every situation harbors the potential for upside; one merely needs to approach it with the appropriate mindset**. This disparity in mindset distinguishes administrative project managers from true project leaders. Irrespective of the circumstances, a project leader consistently seeks alternative perspectives to reframe problems, ultimately yielding superior outcomes. It demands the courage to set aside preconceived notions and consider different contexts or approaches.

SECTION 3

Innovation and Project Initiation

One of the most challenging aspects of project management is the initial phase of getting started. Unless there is a funded mandate with a clearly defined scope, launching a project can be more difficult than actually delivering it. This holds true whether you are a start-up seeking to pitch your ideas to investors or an individual within a large organization requesting resources. While the process of getting started may not follow a linear path, in this section we will explore various techniques that can significantly enhance effectiveness.

[Image by Tumisu from Pixabay]

Understanding Your Customer

Early in my career I used to think that the idea of being customer-centric was somewhat abstract and a little awkward. That is, until I actually started doing actual customer research. One of the first research activities I ever participated in was related to home cleaning. Initially, I approached this assignment with a youthful sense of arrogance, believing it to be a futile use of time. I distinctly remember telling myself, "I've been cleaning things all these years, so I have a pretty good grasp of what it entails." I couldn't have been more mistaken.

Our research participant resided in a two-bedroom apartment with her husband and toddler. After exchanging pleasantries and overcoming initial awkwardness, we delved into our conversation. I began with a simple query: "Could you please show me where you keep your cleaning supplies?" From there, we engaged in a dialogue about each product, exploring reasons for its presence, specific usage areas, and frequency of use. Initially, no groundbreaking insights emerged. I caught myself smugly affirming, "Yes, Windex is truly effective for cleaning windows."

However, something remarkable transpired when we entered her bathroom. It was a small space, entirely tiled, and impeccably clean from top to bottom. Intrigued, I inquired about her cleaning routine. That's when the woman began to unravel emotionally, confessing that she spent one hour each day meticulously cleaning this bathroom. She revealed that she was a smoker but refused to smoke in front of her child. Consequently, multiple times a day, she sought solace in the bathroom, where she would smoke a cigarette with the fan on. Cleaning wasn't a mere functional process, as I had assumed. For her, it represented a complex interplay of emotions intertwined with love, guilt, moral obligation, and an unwavering desire to be a good mother, despite the inherent flaws that come with being human. In short, I was overwhelmed by how limited my understanding was regarding how and why people used cleaning products. This realization sparked a genuine curiosity within me, one that has continued to serve me well.

Importantly, I discovered that engaging in conversations about products and services need not be an awkward endeavor. While some individuals possess a natural aptitude for such discussions (I am not one of them), others may require a more structured approach. One tool I highly recommend is a "discussion guide." As the name suggests, it serves as an outline to facilitate conversations aimed at acquiring knowledge about a particular subject. I favor a general structure, which I've outlined below:

1. **Establish a Learning Objective:** Determine if you seek general information or if there are specific insights you aim to gather.
2. **Identify your Audience:** Define the individuals you wish to engage with and the rationale behind your selection. Remember, sometimes better insights can be gleaned from individuals who do not currently use your product or service, or who may even harbor reservations towards it.
3. **Provide a Short Introduction:** When meeting with someone, introduce yourself, explain the purpose of your discussion, and outline how their input can empower you to enact meaningful changes. People are generally more inclined to offer constructive feedback when they know you possess the authority to implement improvements.
4. **Begin by Letting them Talk**: Initiate the conversation with open-ended questions that encourage individuals to elucidate their relationship with a product, service, or situation. This approach enables them to provide context, feel more at ease, and showcase their knowledge. For example, if you wish to understand how people use their phones, you might inquire, "Tell me about when and where you use your phone?" During the conversation, follow up with "Why do you?"

questions, which often serve as smooth transitions into other related topics you wish to explore. Note that these questions should not be aimed at passing judgment; rather, they should facilitate understanding and allow the individuals to share their experiences.

5. **Understand Likes and Dislikes:** It can be valuable to explore extremes by asking individuals about the aspects they appreciate most and least about a particular subject. Follow up with "Why?" to gain deeper insights. This approach helps establish the upper and lower bounds of their preferences.
6. **Delve into Specifics:** Once a rapport has been established and contextual information has been gathered, you can delve into more specific topics. This can relate to particular features, functions, processes, concepts, ideas, and so forth. For instance, if you are developing a mobile phone app, you could present them with mock-ups of the app to elicit their feedback.
7. **Give them the Final Word:** Occasionally, people may hold back important insights. Therefore, at the conclusion of the conversation, it is beneficial to ask, "Is there anything else you would like me to know?" This allows individuals to conclude the discussion on their own terms. Some of the most valuable insights often emerge at this stage.
8. **Express Gratitude:** Acknowledge that everyone's time is valuable, and thank the participants for generously sharing their perspectives. Show them the respect they deserve.
9. **Document your Insights:** Remember to capture the insights gleaned from the conversation. If you didn't take notes during the discussion, jot down key points immediately afterward while the conversation remains fresh in your mind.

By embracing this structure, you can become a customer research guru, enhancing your understanding of how and why people engage with your products and services.

The Concept of Concepts

It is likely that you, or someone within your network, has a brilliant idea for a project, product, or service. However, an idea remains just that—an idea—until deliberate action is taken to bring it to life. Unfortunately, most individuals never progress beyond the idea stage. This usually leads to one of two scenarios:

1. Overwhelmed by the task at hand, people eventually give up.
2. Fueled by initial excitement, individuals dive straight into costly activities, many of which prove unnecessary and unproductive.

Concepting offers a structured approach that strikes a balance between these two extremes. It is a technique that avoids overwhelming you while keeping your focus on the "right" activities necessary to swiftly propel a new endeavor forward. The goal of concepting is simple: to **quickly reach the point of "kNOw."** This means you either:

1. "Know" that you have a valuable idea and possess insights on how to advance it.
2. Realize that it's a "NO"—an idea lacking value that should be put on hold.

Let's consider an example. Imagine you have a friend who claims to have an incredible product idea that came to them after a late-night snacking mishap. They want to start selling chocolate-covered frozen pickles conveniently packaged in bite-sized portions. According to them, it's a life-changing culinary experience!

This is where concepting comes into play. Instead of immediately dismissing the idea as crazy or investing in costly development without having an indicator of its potential success , you can start by asking, "How can we quickly reach the point of 'kNOw'?"

Here's how it works: a concept typically encapsulates key insights about the idea on paper, similar to the main "ingredients" in a new project recipe.

These insights generally include six items:

1. A definition of the **Unmet Need** from the potential customer's perspective.
2. An overview of the **Proposed Solution** to address their unmet need.
3. Supporting **Evidence** of why your solution will work and why it outperforms other options.
4. **Cost or Pricing** estimation.
5. A supporting **Visual or Mock-up**.
6. Optional: a headline or associated **Selling Copy**.

To illustrate, let's have a little fun and see how this comes to life with the frozen pickle concept example on the next page.

** Concept Example **

The Power of Sour: That's a Healthy Sweet Treat!

Nothing beats the sour taste of a crisp dill pickle. It's the perfect addition to any meal. As a working mom on the go, I crave something sweet and sour to get me through the day. Regular dill pickles are messy and candy bars don't fit my healthy lifestyle. There has to be a better option!

Introducing Chompy's Chocko Pickle Bites!

We lovingly select the highest quality dill pickles, straight from the barrel, and cut them into bite-sized circles. After flash freezing each mouth-watering morsel, we coat them in three layers of the finest chocolate imported from the town of Aire-Sur-La-Lys in Belgium. The result is a cool, delicious treat straight from your freezer that is healthy and satisfying.

We offer three mouthwatering flavors, including:

- Belgian Milk Chocolate with Habanero Pepper Flakes
- Triple Dark Chocolate Dream
- White Chocolate with Garlic Chunks

Unlike other snacks, you can trust that Chompy's Chocko Pickle Bites are Kosher and responsibly sourced from fair trade pickle farms.

As part of our "Boomerangs of Hope Foundation," a portion of the proceeds from every purchase will go towards programs supporting indigenous cucumber farmers off the Northern coast of Australia.

Chomp on down! You can find Chocko-Pickle Bites in the freezer of your favorite health food store in 6-ounce "Snack Packs" priced at $1.95 and 36-ounce "Chompy Packs" priced at $8.95.

** End Concept Example **

Once the concept is documented, you gain a powerful research tool that enables you to take immediate action, without spending any money. By emphasizing the six key elements, your concept establishes the foundation for clarifying important aspects such as:

- Context on "what" the product is
- Potential target audience
- Pricing for financial analysis
- A starting point for exploring distribution and sales strategies
- Advertising and communication approaches
- A basis for competitive market comparisons

With this in mind, you can then adopt a scientific mindset. A good initial step is to establish "success criteria" for the concept before sharing it. These criteria require validation before proceeding. Well-designed criteria will help address the central question: "Is this a project or idea worth investing additional time and money in?" Common criteria for a new product concept like Chompy's Chocko Pickle Bites might include:

- The percentage of people who would consider purchasing the product or service
- Profitability potential
- Estimated market size
- Production costs and distribution complexity

Once clear success criteria are in place, you can begin sharing the concept with others. It's beneficial to outline questions and refine the idea based on their feedback. In addition to addressing the success criteria, these questions can guide you in advancing the concept. Example questions to answer might include:

- How likely would you be to buy or use this product?

- How would you describe this product to a friend?
- (Hide the pricing) Then ask, "How much would you expect a product like this to cost?"
- What do you like about the potential product or service?
- What don't you like about the product or service?
- What could we do to improve the product or service?
- Who do you think would be interested in this product or service?
- What other products or services would you compare this to?

Taking notes along the way is essential. Challenge yourself to engage at least 25 individuals in discussions about the new product or service. This will establish a valuable collection of key insights and inputs.

Now, let's return to how this enables planning clear next steps. Using the example of Chompy's Chocko Pickles, we can illustrate how to reach the point of "kNOw." After sharing the concept with various individuals representing the target audience, only three outcomes are likely:

1. **The Success Criteria are Met or Exceeded**. You "Know" you have a viable product or service idea, which serves as a foundation for advancing the project.
2. **Responses are Mixed**. You can explore concept variations, such as different flavors, ingredients, or prices, to see if they yield greater success before scope is locked down and you commit costly resources.
3. The success **Criteria are Not Met**, resulting in the project being a "NO" go.

The great thing is that all three outcomes are based on data and actionable insights. It's not a matter of personal opinions clashing;

instead, it helps maintain relationships, focus, and cost efficiency.

You can develop concepts for almost any type of project to accelerate alignment, understanding, and support. They can play a central role in clarifying the project's scope.

Overcoming the "Transformation" Hype

The term "transformation" seems to be ubiquitous these days. However, here's a little secret: by simply inserting the word "transformation" into any project title, you significantly increase the likelihood of garnering support or funding. Let's take a practical example. Suppose you have a project involving the replacement of broken or worn-out toilets. Just label it as a "bathroom transformation," and I guarantee you can charge double. But, I digress.

At one point my primary job was to identify emerging technologies, start-ups, or business models that had the potential to help our organization grow. My days were filled with meetings with venture capitalists, startup founders, angel investors, academics, and a diverse array of fascinating individuals. Yes, I even met with a PhD software developer who wore moon boots and a wooden staff strapped to his back. Anyway, my objective was to seek innovative ways to solve existing problems and gain insights into challenges we hadn't even recognized.

During one of these meetings, I found myself in the offices of the venture capital firm Andreessen Horowitz. Their portfolio includes notable companies such as Facebook, Github, Box, Dollar Shave Club, Instagram, Oculus, Lyft, Slack, Zenefits, and more. It's worth mentioning that their tagline was "software is eating the world."

Interestingly, what stuck with me the most from that meeting was the sight of original photographs of hydrogen bomb tests from the 1950s adorning small alcoves in their lobby. Naturally, I pondered, "What kind of organization showcases original photos of hydrogen bomb tests in their lobby?" I filed this question away for further reflection.

Fast forward to the present, and "Transformation Offices" are springing up in corporate headquarters everywhere. My news feeds overflow with a deluge of articles buzzing with the latest catchphrases like artificial intelligence, machine learning, big data, blockchain, and, my all-time favorite, the cloud.

Here's the truth: I have yet to witness a company undergo a "transformation" that truly lives up to the hype. Most transformation initiatives are merely incremental, involving process improvements, the adoption of new technologies, or responses to competitive threats. While this work is undoubtedly valuable, it rarely results in a truly transformed company.

Curiously, the question of "why the hydrogen bomb test photos?" has persisted in my mind, and gradually, an answer has materialized. An organization that proudly displays original photos of hydrogen bomb tests is one that harbors no attachments to the past. It's an organization that embraces the inherent destructive, disruptive, and creative energies that technology embodies, with the intention of forging a different and, hopefully, better future.

Venture capitalists like Andreessen Horowitz, managing vast portfolios of diverse companies, enjoy the luxury of operating without the same constraints as established businesses. They can make multiple "bets on the future" by spreading their risks across numerous ventures. The success of one investment can offset the losses incurred by countless others. Established businesses, on the other hand, typically cannot adopt such an approach.

While numerous books have been written on the topic, I firmly believe that the main challenge for established businesses seeking transformation can be summed up by the Zen saying, "**the sword cannot cut itself.**"

This is precisely why you will never come across an article about Sears revolutionizing retail by taking their catalog online or Kodak transforming photography by digitizing the process of taking, processing, and sharing photos socially. Genuine transformation demands embracing the destructive side of the equation. Pursuing the future often entails dismantling existing business models—the sword cutting itself, akin a hydrogen bomb. This explains why Jeff Bezos recently stated, "I predict one day Amazon will fail. Amazon will go bankrupt. If you look at large companies, their lifespans tend to be 30-plus years, not a hundred-plus years."

This brings us to the fundamental challenge of transformations. If you find yourself in an established business and you anticipate disruption within your industry, what options are available to you? Is establishing a "Transformation Office" the solution? Should you invest in cutting-edge technology or acquire start-ups?

Unfortunately, the challenge is not as straightforward as creating a new organization or pursuing the latest technology. It primarily revolves around talent, culture, and leadership. Navigating this complex problem is undoubtedly arduous but not insurmountable. Drawing from my experience, I've identified four general paths that can be pursued concurrently, without losing sight of your day-to-day operations.

1. **Technology-led Improvements:** In the not-too-distant past, technology was viewed as an enabler. The "business" would identify a need, and the "information technology" function would initiate a project to address it. This approach needs to be reversed. Market-savvy technology-oriented leaders must demonstrate what's possible and then collaborate with the business to implement it. This reorientation encapsulates what most organizations are striving for with digital transformation. The biggest barriers here are culture, outdated organizational models, and the scarcity of market-savvy IT leaders.

2. **Rapid Competitive Response:** In today's landscape, competitors can emerge rapidly from unexpected quarters. Even traditionally "stable" industries like razor blades or mattresses are witnessing the rise of disruptive, small-scale competitors posing genuine threats. Addressing this requires

infusing agility into the organization. Several companies have invested in cross-functional project teams, lightweight infrastructure, and externally focused leaders to mobilize swift responses to competitive threats. For instance, Best Buy successfully countered Amazon's next-day shipping by offering ship-from-store capabilities. This endeavor entailed a cross-functional effort spanning retail operations, logistics, e-commerce, accounting, and more to digitally transform the delivery function. They began with small-scale testing in a handful of stores and rapidly expanded it across the entire business.

3. **Diversified Partnerships:** Joy's law aptly summarizes this approach: "no matter who you are, most of the smartest people work for someone else." To succeed, businesses must cultivate diverse external partner networks. The objective is to gain insights into new threats or opportunities while tapping into external talent to experiment with emerging capabilities. Often, this necessitates establishing a dedicated group within the organization to nurture these partnerships. It is crucial to understand that these relationships are not transactional vendor arrangements and generally cannot be delegated to purchasing organizations. Examples of such initiatives include Unilever Ventures, P&G Connect and Develop, Johnson and Johnson Innovation, and others.

4. **Research and Disruption** (the new R&D): This path is challenging to explain and pursue. It revolves around taking a leading role in shaping the future of an industry. Elon Musk serves as an excellent example of this approach, being at the forefront of disrupting transportation with endeavors such as Tesla, Space-X, self-driving automobiles, ride-sharing services, hyperloop, and the aptly named Boring Company. By leading disruption across various facets of the transportation industry, even if some ventures ultimately fail, it becomes difficult to be left behind. This approach entails existing businesses pursuing concepts that may undermine

> their current operations—a scenario where the sword cuts itself. Jim Hackett's decision to pursue "mobility services" at Ford serves as a real-time example of how challenging this can be. It demands leadership capable of resisting internal and external forces content with the status quo.

For businesses to survive and thrive, embracing elements of transformation becomes imperative. It ultimately involves overcoming internal resistance to change, including the destructive aspects. Recognizing this truth represents one of the initial steps on the path to success. And if all else fails, consider displaying a few photos of atomic bombs going off to spark some lively conversations.

Making the Case for Open Innovation

One of the most exhilarating projects I led was establishing a technology innovation office in the heart of Silicon Valley for an $80 billion multinational company. The mere idea of such an endeavor conjures images of trendy loft spaces, exposed brick walls, tech-savvy programmers in hoodies, and well-stocked kitchens. However, our reality was quite different. Our office was a modest 300-square-foot room with a conference table, a small alcove for laptops and a printer, and a high-end video-conferencing unit. The only glamorous aspect was the partially blocked view of Market Street in San Francisco and a coffee station that was shared by the other tenants.. Our team consisted of myself and two individuals from other business units within the company. Despite our small team and basic office setup, we achieved remarkable results. Here's how we did it.

Traditional approaches to innovation suggest that companies should invest in their own internal research and development projects. While this holds true for highly proprietary or core competency areas, even in those cases, meaningful innovation relies on the contributions of communities of professionals sharing their experiences, knowledge, and insights. After all, even a PhD researcher on your team had to acquire their skills and knowledge somewhere.

Consider the fact that the world's population exceeds 7 billion people, with thousands of years of recorded history. No matter what problem you're trying to solve, chances are someone else has already solved it. This realization formed the foundation of our daily work.

Our office served as a hub connecting the "wicked problems" and "big opportunity areas" defined by our company with extensive networks of academics, start-ups, investors, accelerators, non-competitive peer organizations, governmental bodies, research institutes, and more. If individuals believed they could contribute to solving these problems, we organized low-effort proof-of-concept tests to evaluate the viability and scalability of their solutions. If a solution proved viable, we established mutually beneficial agreements and incorporated it into our project portfolio. If not, we maintained those relationships, hoping that new opportunities would arise in the future.

You might wonder, what does this have to do with project management? The answer is simple: effectiveness. **The most successful projects are the ones you never have to undertake**.

Too often projects are initiated with the assumption that something needs to be created when perfectly acceptable solutions already exist. For example, if given enough time, money, and resources, I could lead a project to create a means of transportation to fly from the United States to Asia. However, it is much more effective to simply buy a plane ticket. This is where project managers have an opportunity. A good project manager should always be looking beyond the organization. There are people, knowledge, tools, and capabilities available that can enhance the effectiveness of any project. All it takes is asking the questions, "Who else may have already solved this problem?" and "What can I learn from them?"

Baselining Your Project

During my teenage years I made some dumb decisions. Among the many foolish endeavors on my list was bungee jumping. Luckily, I had the wisdom to jump with a professional guide instead of attempting a "do it yourself" bungee jump from a random bridge. I vividly remember standing on the edge of the platform, several hundred feet above the ground, with a bungee cord securely strapped to my body. After taking a deep breath, I leaped headfirst into the void, only to be snapped back in the same direction. Newton's laws of motion took effect, causing every blood cell in my body to rush into my skull. The price of my five-second adrenaline rush was a 24-hour migraine headache. Thus ended my brief venture into extreme sports.

Now, if there's something I consider even more foolhardy than bungee jumping, it's base jumping. Unlike bungee jumping, base jumping entails leaping off buildings or bridges without the safety of a bungee cord. Instead, one deploys a parachute mid-jump, which, if executed correctly, prevents a catastrophic landing on the ground. However, a minor miscalculation during base jumping can serve as another data point affirming the validity of Darwin's theory of evolution.

So, what does base jumping have to do with project management? I use base jumping as a metaphor for projects that lack "baseline" measures to compare performance against. Failing to establish a baseline is akin to leaping into the unknown without any tethering. Allow me to elaborate.

A baseline refers to a measure or series of measures that define the current or average performance of a process, organization, business, system, and so on. As the name suggests, it serves as a direct "line" connecting your project to quantifiable benefits. These measures may encompass aspects such as defects, costs, sales volume, satisfaction, or any relevant factors specific to your situation. Once the baseline is established, you can assess the potential impact of your project against these measures.

For instance, when baselining a project aimed at improving customer satisfaction, you can compare satisfaction levels before and after project completion. If an improvement is observed, you can claim victory. If there is no discernible improvement, you will at least have a starting point to investigate the reasons why. Conversely, if you engage in base jumping, you essentially leap into the void without any basis for comparison. Consequently, when someone inevitably asks you to demonstrate the value of your work, you will painfully realize the absence of before-and-after measures to confidently showcase your results. A literal "splat!"

Exploring Project Benefits

There is a famous quote by Theodore Levitt, a professor at Harvard Business School, which states, "People don't want to buy a quarter-inch drill bit, they want a quarter-inch hole!" This quote highlights the need for businesses to shift their focus from what they produce internally to what the customer is trying to achieve. By continuously understanding and addressing the customer's goals, businesses can adapt and stay relevant. However, I would argue that people are not even interested in the quarter-inch hole itself. More often, the quarter-inch hole serves as a means to an end, such as building, creating, or repairing something else.

This raises the challenging topic of defining project benefits and determining what the project is truly trying to accomplish. In my experience, many project managers primarily concentrate on the "drill bit" – the deliverables and execution. This inclination is unsurprising since their role often revolves around delivery and implementation. Nevertheless, it is essential for all stakeholders to play their part in ensuring that the project delivers the desired outcome. If the project veers off course, it is crucial to regroup, even if it means adjusting the original scope or deliverables, to ensure the desired outcome is achieved.

To assist teams in managing this challenge and minimizing theoretical benefit debates, I recommend a simple approach: the **"So You Can"** or "SYC" technique. Here's how it works:

1. Identify the core deliverables of the project.
2. Create a statement by appending "so you can..." after each deliverable.
3. Continue this process until you reach the highest-level benefit.

4. This will provide a "benefit spectrum" to explore at an appropriate level.

For example, let's say you are leading a project team responsible for developing an eCommerce module on a company's website. Your SYC might unfold as follows:

We are providing a new eCommerce function on the website.

- So you can list our products online.
- So you can provide customers with another channel to purchase our products.
- So you can attract new and different buyers who prefer online shopping over in-store experiences.
- So you can match the capabilities offered by our competitors.
- So you can increase sales.
- So you can improve profitability.
- So you can generate more value for shareholders.

As you can see, this technique primarily serves as a brainstorming exercise to identify potential benefits stemming from the deliverables. It is up to the team to subsequently identify and validate the benefits that are most relevant.

Once the benefits are identified, the team faces the challenge of:

1. Predicting the likely benefits.
2. Determining how to measure these benefits.
3. Identifying potential measures and areas to explore and comprehend. For instance:
    - Will the product attract new customers or cannibalize existing ones?

- Can the increase in sales be directly attributed to this new function?
- How much additional sales are required to justify the cost of implementing the new function?

By following this process, your project will be better equipped to understand, measure, and communicate its true value.

Shiny Projects vs. Clear Problems

Everyone is drawn to shiny objects. From a young age, we're instinctively captivated by the allure of new things. The phenomenon of "unboxing videos" confirms this undeniable truth. I, too, must admit that I thoroughly enjoy the thrill of acquiring something new, unpacking it, and putting it to the test.

However, there lies a challenge. Shiny objects can often lead to wasteful projects. They are frequently initiated based on the allure of new technologies, business models, management methods, or consultant pitches adorned with the latest buzzwords. While there are instances where these can be beneficial, there is also a potential downside to consider.

Allow me to illustrate this point. I once collaborated with a business leader who aimed to automate a critical business process. He articulated his intention to sponsor a project to build an artificial intelligence (AI) solution to enhance the process. Why? Simply because AI was the latest trend among leading companies, and he had come across several articles endorsing its merits. After delving deeper into the problem, we discovered that employing artificial intelligence was excessive. The process could be automated using simpler and more cost-effective methods.

This scenario exemplifies the trap we can fall into when fixating on solutions without thoroughly exploring the underlying problem. It's not a novel phenomenon. Even Albert Einstein was famously quoted as saying, "If I had an hour to solve a problem, I'd spend 55 minutes thinking about the problem, and 5 minutes thinking about solutions."

Critics might argue that Einstein was mistaken about various matters, including the cosmological constant, so his recommended approach to problem solving may also be flawed. That's a fair point. However, based on my experience, I'm inclined to give Einstein the benefit of the doubt on this one.

With that in mind, when you find yourself irresistibly drawn to a shiny object, I recommend taking a step back to examine the problem at hand. A simple technique I employ is what I refer to as the **"how might we?" problem statement**. To better understand its workings, let's revisit the earlier example of the business leader initiating an AI project to enhance a business process. Instead of immediately leaping to a solution, we would begin by precisely defining the problem. It could be framed as follows: "How might we decrease the time our team spends on process XYZ by 50%, while reducing defects by at least 25%, with an investment of $15,000 or less?"

By encapsulating the desired outcome, specifying measurable success metrics, and incorporating constraints within a single statement, this straightforward technique paves the way for exploring a multitude of diverse solutions. Various practical approaches to problem definition are elaborated upon in greater detail within the Design Thinking methodology developed by IDEO and Stanford University.

Undoubtedly, problem definition is an invaluable tool. However, it's crucial to recognize that there are two sides to the equation. We mustn't overlook the fact that shiny objects possess the power to help us envision new possibilities and perceive problems from previously unexplored angles. They contribute to the zeitgeist that propels innovation and progress. Thus, rather than shunning shiny objects outright, adopting a balanced approach and resisting the allure of a singular solution is advisable.

SECTION 4

Programs, Portfolios, and PMO Organizations

Managing a single project is a challenging endeavor on its own. However, when faced with the task of handling multiple projects simultaneously, complexities significantly increase. As you undertake larger endeavors, it is inevitable that you will encounter a multitude of organizational challenges. In this section we will explore these dynamics in order to help increase your effectiveness as a project manager and overall leader.

[Image by Arek Socha from Pixabay]

The Story of Why PMOs Fail and How to Avoid It

Did you know that according to research, at least 50% or more of Project Management Office (PMO) organizations fail within the first 3 or 4 years of inception? A scholarly article from the Project Management Institute provides extensive details on this issue (Spalek, 2014). It even includes a visually appealing 5-circle Venn diagram for those who appreciate such things.

While numerous researchers have compiled lengthy lists of contributing factors derived through surveys, I believe they fail to tell it how it really is. In my experience, the main reason PMOs fail often boils down to one thing: a lack of flexibility.

Understanding the Lifecycle of a PMO

To grasp the magnitude of the problem, it's important to understand the typical lifecycle of a new PMO before it fails. It usually unfolds as follows:

In the beginning, there is a wave of enthusiasm. Frustrated by poor results, people passionately discuss the benefits of having project professionals, certifications, the importance of best practices, and the potential for improvement. A sponsor appoints a respected leader who begins assembling a group of project management-oriented individuals. If we imagine the late 1920s, it's as if people in their crisply pressed suits and flapper dresses are joyfully singing "Happy Days are Here Again."

To initiate progress, the PMO leaders conduct workshops to establish standards, provide training classes, introduce tools, and develop templates. Without a doubt, everyone nods in agreement, recognizing the value of these initiatives.

Citations: Spalek, S. (2014). Do you really want your PMO to survive? Paper presented at PMI® Global Congress 2014—EMEA, Dubai, United Arab Emirates. Newtown Square, PA: Project Management Institute.

Once there's agreement, the real work begins. Individuals are assigned to lead significant project and things start happening. Status reports are exchanged, the tools and standards prove helpful, and projects start moving forward with greater levels of success.

Since large projects usually take time to deliver, at least a year goes by without much disruption. During this time, project managers build strong relationships with leaders in their respective areas or functions. And then, in a strange but predictable turn of events, the PMO project managers start assimilating within the specific area of the company they support. They begin identifying more with the function or area sponsors than with the PMO.

Another year passes, and the executive team returns to the PMO, seeking assistance with new important projects. After all, that's what the PMO is supposed to help with. Eager to contribute, PMO leadership starts searching for project managers to meet the demand. To their surprise, they discover that reallocating their best project managers to new initiatives is extremely challenging. Sponsors are reluctant to let go of their skilled project managers, and those project managers, who have become ingrained within their respective functions, are resistant to moving to a new area.

To avoid causing unrest, most PMO leaders are left with two undesirable options. One is bad, and the other is even worse. They can either recommend hiring more people to meet the increased demand or pull resources from existing projects. While this might be acceptable initially, the second or third time the PMO requests additional resources or reallocates embedded project managers, executive leadership starts having second thoughts.

The Tipping Point

At this stage, the sponsoring executive teams typically contemplate the following logic:

- "Our project management standards are already defined. People are familiar with the best practices, so why are we burdened with the costly overhead of someone managing these practices? It seems like low-value work to me."
- "Whenever I request PMO support, it's slow, and I often face demands for more resources or the reallocation of talent from other important initiatives. Why should we go through the hassle of a bureaucratic exercise when I can simply hire project managers independently?"
- "Hold on a minute. We already have competent project managers embedded within our various functions. Let's eliminate the central PMO overhead, allow project managers to report within their respective functions, and be done with it. We'll save some money and still achieve the same results. And if we need additional talent, the functional leaders are more than capable of hiring within their teams."

And just like that, the PMO disappears, and executives proudly boast about cost savings resulting from the latest reduction in force (RIF) initiative. Of course, five years pass, new leaders enter the organization, collective amnesia sets in, and the entire cycle starts afresh. Queue the band to play "Happy Days are Here Again" once more.

Now, I'm not suggesting that this is the exact story for every PMO. However, after speaking with numerous leaders across the industry and personally working with various companies, I have noticed some common themes. The primary theme is that PMO failure is not the result of improperly applying specific project management tools or processes; **it is a failure of organizational design and stakeholder management**.

How to Break the Cycle

Recognizing the unique challenge that project organizations face, it is crucial to address the cycle of PMO failure. Unlike other operational organizations such as accounting, finance, marketing, and operations, project organizations deal with highly variable needs dependent on ever-changing internal and external conditions. Breaking this cycle requires two key actions:

1. Designing the organization for flexibility.
2. Setting clear expectations with executive sponsors and project managers.

While there is no one-size-fits-all approach to organizational design, the visual below outlines core components that contribute to creating a flexible PMO organization. Let's delve into each element and understand how they work together:

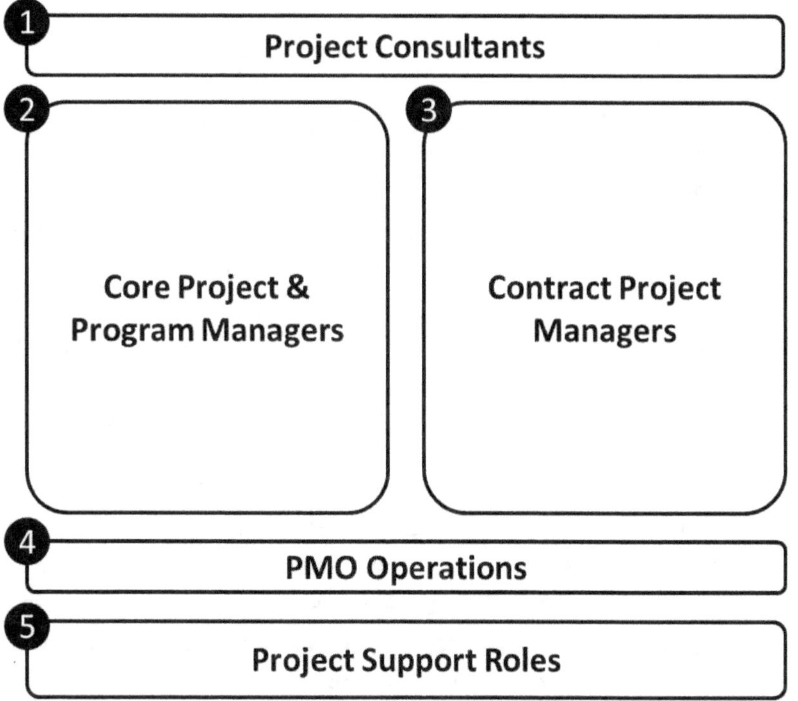

1. **Project Consultants:** Maintain a small group of highly experienced project professionals, ideally consisting of some of your most senior individuals. These PMO team members possess the unique ability to engage with executives, adapt to various scenarios, analyze situations, and excel in project-related tasks. They are akin to special forces in the military, deployed for short-term engagements. Their role involves assessing, accelerating, organizing, and engaging the right resources before moving on.

   These team members are typically engaged for a period of 30, 60, or 90 days, to ensure a constant supply of highly skilled individuals to address emerging needs. This approach enables the PMO to avoid offering a firm "NO" when resources are requested, as new needs continually arise. Moreover, since these team members are the most senior individuals in the project organization, they may have direct or indirect authority over core project and program managers (#2), allowing them to provide practical, experience-based coaching to develop other team members.

2. **Core Project & Program Managers:** This group forms the majority of full-time project professionals within the PMO. Depending on their skill level and experience, these individuals may manage individual projects or highly complex programs. Unlike consultants (#1) or contract project managers (#3), they are typically assigned to high-value projects with longer durations (exceeding three months). This part of the organization tends to be less flexible, but that is acceptable since many large-scale efforts require stability and continuity.

3. **Contract Project Managers:** Establish formal relationships with multiple external contract project management agencies. This ensures the PMO always has the ability to quickly scale up or down the project management workforce. Contract project managers are best deployed for lower-value, lower-

complexity projects, or on larger projects that are already well-organized and simply require maintenance until completion. They can also provide administrative support under the direction of an experienced internal project leader.

By centralizing key agency relationships, PMO Operations (#4) can ensure that contracted organizations adhere to the specific standards of the PMO while monitoring and controlling costs. Furthermore, depending on the structure of these agency relationships, contract project managers who demonstrate high proficiency may be considered for full-time employment, reducing the risks associated with acquiring talent in the open market.

4. **PMO Operations:** The operations team plays a vital role in the organization, albeit they must be incredibly lean to avoid being viewed as too costly. Similar to a symphony conductor, they ensure that all processes work together harmoniously. Their responsibilities include managing demand intake, capacity planning, portfolio planning processes, project reporting, project auditing, training, professional development, defining standards, managing tools or technology platforms, overseeing contract agencies, monitoring KPIs, and more. By maintaining smooth work processes, this team ensures flexibility and continuous optimization of resources.

5. **Project Support Roles:** Depending on the industry, size, or maturity of the organization, the PMO may integrate project support roles to cater to specialized skill sets required at various stages of the project lifecycle. Examples of such roles include Change Managers (providing training, communications, and adoption support), Business Analysts (defining scope, requirements, and business needs), Project Coordinators (offering technical and administrative support to project managers), Relationship or Client Managers (working with executive sponsors to cultivate and ensure the

success of specific projects within the portfolio), and Financial Analysts (overseeing funding allocations, budget performance, and validation of financial benefits).

This Supports a Project Management Career Model

Maintaining these components within the PMO establishes a framework for professional development and career progression. It provides individuals with increasing opportunities for responsibility and growth, creating a sense of belonging and appreciation for their skills. When individuals recognize a clear development path, they are less likely to become entrenched within specific functions, leading to reduced turnover and more professionals willing to build their careers within the PMO. As their project expertise grows, the organization's value potential also increases.

Organizational Design is Only One Part of the Equation

While organizational design addresses the flexibility aspect, it is equally important for PMO leadership to set proper expectations. To achieve this, I recommend that project management organizations establish a simple "engagement plan" directly with project sponsors for each supported project. This plan should be concise, no longer than one page, and include basic items such as resource type, core deliverables, day-to-day responsibilities, expected time commitment, conditions for reassessment or project termination, and clarity that individual assignments are subject to the PMO's discretion, with replacements of similar skill and experience.

By formalizing the engagement plan, the PMO conveys three critical messages:

1. The function is receiving a skilled resource to fulfill an important need rather than a specific person.

2. The tasks, time, and conditions required for completing the engagement are clearly defined, including an exit plan.

3. For the individual project professional, it reinforces that they are part of the PMO team, performing a service on behalf of the organization, rather than being solely supported by the function.

These messages establish the necessary "ground rules" for maintaining the project organization's flexibility and supporting the broader needs of the company or entity.

How to Measure PMO Success

In the realm of project management, the success of a Project Management Office (PMO) lies in its ability to effectively fulfill its purpose. A thriving PMO demonstrates its value by meeting organizational needs and avoiding failure. Evaluating key metrics can serve as a compass, guiding you in the right direction as your organization's requirements evolve. Consider the following measures to assess whether your PMO is on the right track:

1. **Time to Staff New PMO Requests**: Monitor the duration it takes to allocate resources and fulfill new PMO requests promptly. Timely staffing reflects efficiency and agility in meeting project demands.

2. **Number of New Requests Open for More than Two Weeks**: Keep track of the number of newly submitted requests that remain unresolved after two weeks. This metric can help identify bottlenecks and areas for improvement in request processing.

3. **Sponsor Satisfaction with PMO Engagements**: Gauge sponsor satisfaction through a five-point attribute agreement scale. Regularly assess sponsors' perceptions of the PMO's performance and address any concerns or areas for enhancement.

4. **PMO Team Member Satisfaction:** Measure the satisfaction levels of PMO team members using a five-point attribute agreement scale. A content and motivated team contributes

to improved project outcomes and fosters a positive work environment.

5. **Percentage of PMO Engagement in Key Projects/Initiatives**: Determine the PMO's relative market share of initiatives by tracking the percentage of projects or initiatives the PMO actively supports. This metric helps assess the PMO's influence and its alignment with strategic objectives.
6. **Staff Retention and Turnover:** Monitor staff retention rates within the PMO. A high turnover rate may indicate underlying issues such as low morale or inadequate support. Focus on creating a conducive work environment to retain talented individuals.
7. **Audit Results of Standards:** Regularly review and assess the adherence to standards by both contract and internal resources. Conduct thorough audits to ensure compliance and identify areas that require improvement to maintain quality and consistency.
8. **Average Hourly Contractor Rates vs. Industry Benchmarks:** Compare the average hourly rates of contractors engaged by the PMO against industry benchmarks. This analysis helps ensure cost-effectiveness and identifies opportunities for cost optimization.

Lastly, remember the ultimate measure of success: whether or not your PMO continues to exists! Align the PMO's goals and activities with the overall strategic objectives of the organization, ensuring its relevance and contribution to long-term success. And most importantly – stay flexible. With that in mind you'll be equipped to beat the odds.

Cultivating a Value Creation Culture

About six years into my career, I had the opportunity to manage IT organizations across multiple pet food manufacturing facilities. Despite the less-than-pleasant aroma of working in a pet food production facility, I faced a common challenge with my team. We often felt that our hard work went unnoticed and lacked recognition from upper management. Managing or sponsoring around 8 or 9 projects simultaneously, we realized the need for a clear framework to communicate the value we were contributing. Our achievements were often anecdotal, and unfortunately, people tended to focus more on the negatives than the positives.

During that time, my manager approached me to address this issue. He suggested that I organize information from different teams to establish a consistent framework for project communication. Enthusiastically embracing this opportunity, I immediately delved into the task. I gathered essential information about our projects and initiated meetings with finance managers to bring credibility to our project results. Together, we devised a "value creation" framework to be implemented across all sites.

The framework consisted of a comprehensive list of active and completed projects for each site. Active projects featured a "committed value contribution," while completed projects displayed an "actualized value contribution." Both the IT manager and finance manager at each site had to verify the value creation contribution for each project. These contributions would be updated quarterly, and my responsibility was to consolidate them into a comprehensive portfolio.

Our value creation framework was organized into a simple spreadsheet with different benefit categories. All projects were required to define their benefits within the highlighted categories on the next page:

1. Hard Benefits
2. Soft Benefits
3. Strategic Benefits
4. Mandatory Benefits

Let's delve into the description of each benefit category:

Hard Benefits: As the name suggests, these benefits are tangible and quantifiable, directly impacting the bottom line. For instance, a project might reduce the amount of materials needed to produce a product, resulting in a $5 per unit cost reduction. Upon project completion, the actual cost reduction can be validated within the operations. On the other hand, a project could focus on supporting a new product that generates an annual revenue increase of $1,000,000.

Soft Benefits: Similar to hard benefits, soft benefits can be measured or quantified. For example, an application processing department might undertake a project that reduces the daily effort of three employees by 30 minutes each. This can be validated by analyzing the workflows post-project completion and measured monetarily based on 90 minutes of payroll. However, unlike hard benefits, these benefits may not directly affect the bottom line. Instead, it is assumed that the time saved will be allocated to other productive purposes.

Strategic Benefits: Unlike hard or soft benefits, strategic benefits are often challenging to quantify but contribute to the organization's long-term success. These benefits include responding to present or future competitive threats, safeguarding the organization against competitors, or enhancing the organization's flexibility to adapt to changes. A practical example would be producing "value size" products, which reduces purchase frequency and limits opportunities for competitors to sway customers away from our offerings. For an IT organization, a strategic benefit could involve migrating to a new technical platform that better aligns with anticipated future needs.

Mandatory Benefits: These projects are deemed essential and must be completed to meet legal, regulatory, or government mandates. In this context, the deliverable itself is considered the benefit. Examples include updating an organization's accounting information system to comply with SOX (Sarbanes Oxley) requirements or replacing outdated production equipment that no longer meets health and safety standards.

While the value creation framework successfully addressed the need for visibility and support for high-value projects, it had an additional important impact: it fostered a cultural shift. Leaders across all sites began using a common language to explain their projects and were better equipped to identify potential benefits or lack thereof. This improved decision making, prioritization, and limited debates over lower value opportunities.

By implementing the value creation framework, we were able to create a culture that acknowledged and appreciated the value we brought to the organization. It provided a standardized approach for project communication, enabling better alignment and understanding among teams.

Prioritizing Projects

During an interview for a project management position, I was once asked a challenging question: "What would you do if your stakeholders wanted you to deliver multiple projects on accelerated timelines, without enough resources?" My response was straightforward yet practical. I said I would tell them "No." Then I would honestly communicate the constraints and outline realistic options.

In such a situation, there are generally three approaches to consider:

1. **Set Realistic Expectations**: Utilize logical reasoning to explain the limitations posed by the available resources. By providing a clear and honest assessment, stakeholders can better understand the challenges and adjust their expectations accordingly.
2. **Prioritize and Reduce Low Priority Projects**: In order to align the available resources with the demands, it may be necessary to prioritize projects and reduce the number of low priority initiatives. This ensures that the most crucial and impactful projects receive adequate attention and resources.
3. **Request Additional Resources:** If the project requirements cannot be met with the current resource allocation, it is essential to communicate the need for additional resources. By presenting a well-defined business case and demonstrating the potential benefits, it becomes easier to secure the necessary support.

Although my response may not have been well-received by the interviewer, it is important to acknowledge that sometimes saying "No" is necessary. People often have a preference for hearing "Yes" even when they understand the feasibility challenges, as it allows them to avoid making difficult decisions.

Unfortunately, this scenario reflects the reality in almost every organization. The demand for projects always surpasses the available time, money, and personnel. Balancing these constraints is a constant challenge.

To navigate this challenge effectively it's crucial to establish a framework for prioritizing work. I recommend something like this simple model highlighted below.

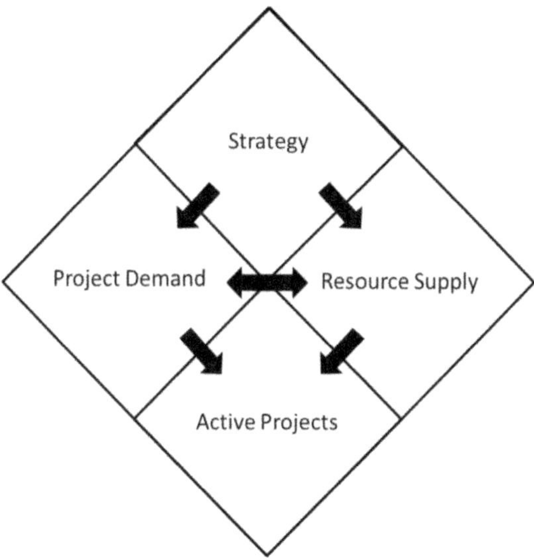

Ideally, every portfolio should be guided by a few simple strategies defined by the leadership. These strategies, in turn, determine project priorities (demand) and the allocation of resources such as money and people (supply). Regular assessment of active projects ensures alignment with organizational goals.

The **primary objective is to maintain equilibrium** by continuously reassessing priorities and reallocating resources in the context of changes in strategy or insights coming from active projects. This ensures that the right resources are dedicated to the right projects, enabling the realization of organizational strategies. Like the conductor of an orchestra, the Project Management Office (PMO) or portfolio leader assumes a central role in guiding the leadership through this delicate balancing act.

In today's culture of instant gratification, it is essential to remember that great leaders are defined by their ability to choose which endeavors not to pursue, allowing their teams to excel in a few selected areas. **Leaders must know when to say "No."** Conversely, project professionals should focus on identifying the conditions necessary for success within the framework, enabling them to confidently say "Yes."

Portfolio Architecture

One of my favorite Johnny Cash songs is called "One Piece at a Time." It tells the story of a man working at a General Motors factory in Detroit, Michigan, where Cadillac luxury cars are made. He devises a plan to steal a part from the assembly line in his lunch box every day, with the intention of eventually having enough parts to build his own Cadillac. This continues for over a decade until he finally gathers all the necessary parts. However, upon assembling the car, he realizes that the entire idea was a disaster. The collected parts, accumulated over a decade, do not fit together properly. The result is an unsightly car that barely functions. In the end, when he proudly takes his wife out for a drive, they become the laughing stock of the town.

Apart from being a fan of Johnny Cash, I appreciate this song because it accurately portrays how most organizations evolve—one piece at a time. Every time I see a dysfunctional organization that song goes through my head. Anyway, I have encountered numerous consulting engagements where teams grapple with issues stemming from outdated or incompatible systems, solutions, services, and teams. When I inquire about the origins of these problems, the common response is, "It just evolved this way over time."

To disentangle such complexities and organize work effectively to prevent future issues, I recommend adopting a "portfolio architecture." The fundamental purpose of this framework is to establish clear relationships among projects, systems, teams, and products or services within an organization. While not a one-size-fits all proposition, this approach facilitates sound decision-making and an example is highlighted on the next page.

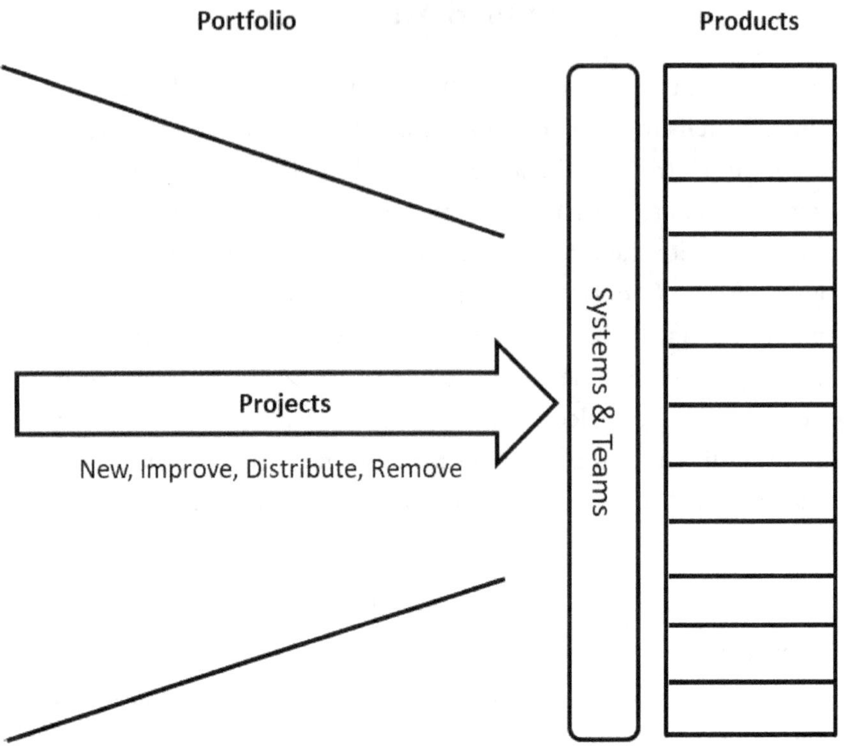

When building the framework, it is best to start from the "outside in." Begin by identifying the various products or services offered by the organization from the customer's perspective. Keep in mind that these don't have to be commercial products, but can also be internal processes or services delivered within the company.

Next, document how the various systems and teams relate to these products. Once this is documented you will have the appropriate structure to prioritize projects within the portfolio, hence the name "portfolio architecture." Each project will have one or several relationships with the architecture. Typically, over 90% of the projects within the portfolio will relate to the architecture in the following ways:

- Create a **NEW** product, team, or system.
- Deliver an **IMPROVEMENT** to an existing product, team, or supporting system.
- **DISTRIBUTE** a pre-existing product or system to a new audience.
- **REMOVE** a product, team, or system.

Understanding these relationships is essential to minimizing the unplanned evolution that occurs "one piece at a time." The framework equips leaders with the visibility needed to identify opportunities for creating value. Here are some common areas to explore:

1. **Look for Product Redundancies**: This highlights opportunities for removal, reducing costs and complexity.
2. **Identify Scale Opportunities:** These often arise when systems and teams can expand their support to multiple products.
3. **Explore New Distribution Channels**: Introducing an existing product to a new audience is often easier than creating an entirely new product.
4. **Try Different Ways to Categorize Groups of Products**: This may enable you to position new products for a different audience.
5. **Highlight and Prioritize Improvements:** Look for opportunities that affect the largest parts of the framework or create the most pain-points for customers.

By adopting a portfolio architecture approach, organizations can proactively address issues caused by the accumulation of disparate elements over time. This enables better decision-making, cost reduction, and acceleration of the highest value creating opportunities.

SECTION 5

Career Advice for Aspiring Project Leaders

One of the remarkable aspects of project management is its inclusivity. It is a profession that is open to individuals from diverse educational backgrounds, irrespective of whether they hold a PhD or haven't even completed a high school education. The demand for effective project management transcends such distinctions. I firmly believe that anyone with a strong sense of purpose and a willingness to learn can excel as a project manager. What truly matters is investing the time and gaining valuable experience. Keeping this in mind, the content in this section delves into various topics to assist individuals aspiring to progress in their personal and professional lives.

[Image by Markus Kammermann from Pixabay]

Maintain at Least Three Important Goals

This topic may seem obvious, but its importance cannot be overstated. Knowing what you want is essential. Countless times, I've engaged in coaching conversations with individuals who lacked clarity about their true desires. Far too often, people passively approach their professional development, failing to proactively define their aspirations. When asked thought-provoking questions like "Where do you see yourself in two years?" or "Five years from now?", it is often disheartening when people say, "I don't know."

For me personally, as I continually pursued greater challenges, I ensured that my goals possessed two vital characteristics:

1. **Specificity:** Each goal was defined with precision, leaving no room for ambiguity.
2. **Achievability:** While ambitious, my goals were realistically attainable, driving me towards success.

I strongly recommend everyone to maintain a concise set of personal or professional goals. In my experience, it is beneficial to focus on a limited number of goals at any given time—usually around three. Here are some examples of goals I have set throughout my career:

- Earn a degree specializing in computers and business.
- Gain hands-on experience with ERP (enterprise resource planning) systems.
- Live and work abroad.
- Learn a foreign language.
- Work in a startup environment.
- Assume responsibility for a business's profit and loss.
- Become a consultant.
- Work in Silicon Valley.
- Obtain a project management certification.
- Complete my MBA.
- Write a book!
- And so on...

You'll notice that these goals, while not overly complex, reflect personal aspirations at different stages of my career. To make them tangible, I carry a tiny slip of paper in my wallet where I jot down my goals. There is something empowering about putting pen to paper—it solidifies the commitment to pursue what you truly want.

If you haven't done so already, I encourage you to put this into practice. It costs nothing. Amidst the countless publications on career development and self-help books, simply dedicating yourself to a few personal goals, and ensuring that you are working towards them every day, can make all the difference.

The Two Feet Principle

During my childhood, one of my favorite pastimes was exploring the woods. I vividly recall the creek in our backyard that I loved to venture into. It was teeming with fossils, salamanders, tadpoles, and various other fascinating discoveries. Whenever I attempted to cross the creek, I had to carefully step from one rock to another, ensuring I stayed on stable ground to avoid falling into the water. I would always keep one foot firmly planted on a secure rock while testing the stability of the next one with my other foot. Once I confirmed its reliability, I would shift my weight onto it and prepare to advance to the next rock.

This simple childhood experience serves as a perfect metaphor for our careers. To prevent failure, or in this case, falling into the water, it is crucial to keep one foot firmly grounded in a position of strength that we know will support us. Simultaneously, to progress and develop professionally, we must always look ahead to identify where we can place our other foot and cultivate new strengths.

This perspective shapes my approach to considering new assignments, projects, or challenges. Whatever opportunity arises, it should leverage a strength, ensuring a reliable foundation to rely upon when faced with difficulties. However, it should also present unfamiliar challenges, enabling new experiences that foster growth and development.

The Yin and Yang of Careers

When contemplating careers, I maintain the belief that there are two fundamental orientations that shape our experiences. These orientations can be likened to the concepts of yin and yang, representing opposite yet interconnected characteristics—breadth and depth. A career focused on depth revolves around cultivating a high level of expertise within a specific field. This may include specialized professions like doctors, professors, scientists, engineers, or military officers. Over time, those who choose this path continuously develop and elevate themselves within their chosen discipline. Personal fulfillment and accomplishment are derived from undertaking increasingly complex challenges that demonstrate mastery of a particular skill set.

On the other hand, a career focused on breadth embraces variety and novel experiences. While individuals may undoubtedly develop some depth in a specific area, personal fulfillment arises from pursuing challenges associated with entirely new endeavors. As time progresses, the breadth of experience offers valuable insights that prepare individuals for dealing with unfamiliar situations. Examples of careers that prioritize breadth may include consultants, entrepreneurs, brand managers, or project managers. For these professionals, every day brings new challenges that they may or may not be fully equipped to handle. Nevertheless, it is often the sense of uncertainty that makes their work exhilarating.

It is worth noting that these paths are not mutually exclusive. Some individuals gravitate towards the extremes, while others adopt a more balanced or middle path approach. Moreover, one's inclination towards depth or breadth may evolve throughout their career. However, being honest with oneself about the preferred path serves as a helpful framework for making decisions regarding personal development and growth.

What Kind of Risks are You Taking?

Do you recall how many times you crashed your bicycle before learning to ride? Can you even remember how many times you fell down before learning how to walk? Probably not. During our younger years, failure and learning are synonymous.

However, somewhere along life's journey, things change. Despite the popular mantras of "fail fast" or "creating a culture where it's okay to fail," many professionals no longer associate failure with learning. Instead, failure becomes synonymous with weakness or incompetence. This stigma leads us to take fewer risks and, consequently, limit our own potential.

Learning from Failure

I had the experience of being part of a failed start-up, and I wouldn't trade that experience for anything. I learned more during my time in a failed business than I ever did from MBA classes on entrepreneurship, marketing, or management.

For context, our business concept revolved around a noble purpose. Museums and art galleries allowed us to collect used shipping crates that were destined for landfills. Research showed that approximately 2 million of these crates were thrown away every year, wasting precious resources such as water, trees, and landfill space, as well as contributing to air pollution through unnecessary transportation.

Most of these crates were custom-crafted to securely transport high-value pieces of art. Our idea was to collect the crates, refurbish them, and offer them for resale and reuse online. We also established B2B partnerships with art handlers to provide our products as an ecologically friendly and cost-effective alternative to traditional crates.

Our primary business hypothesis was that there would be a "middle market" of environmentally conscious customers interested in purchasing these crates. However, after launching the business, we quickly discovered the following market dynamics:

- The high end of the market preferred new custom crates, as they were hesitant to use used crates for valuable artwork.
- The low end of the market couldn't afford the shipping costs, which often exceeded $500 due to the crates' weight.
- The middle market we anticipated failed to materialize. Despite extensive marketing and direct sales efforts, we only experienced a trickle of sales.

Undoubtedly, there are few things more disheartening than investing your heart and soul into a business, only to fall short. Nevertheless, the lessons learned along the way are invaluable.

Allow me to share some insights from my experience:

1. **Focus on Taking Action**: One thing we did exceptionally well was swiftly getting our store online and making our products available for purchase. We avoided excessive overthinking and, once operational, continuously iterated and improved based on the feedback received from the actual market.
2. **Market Research has its Limitations:** Before launching, we dedicated significant time to speaking with individuals in the art community. They all expressed interest in affordable, environmentally friendly shipping solutions. They were ecstatic when we presented our concept to them. However, when it came time to actually buy our products, they were nowhere to be found. This serves as a classic example of researcher bias, wherein individuals may express favorable sentiments merely to be polite.
3. **Define your Criteria for Success**: Prior to launching, we established a small set of goals. We all agreed that if specific benchmarks were not met, we would reassess and potentially abandon the venture. This clear definition of success aided

decision-making, especially during emotionally charged moments.

4. **Separate Business Failure from Personal Failure.** When you invest significant time, effort, and capital into something, it naturally becomes personal. This holds true for start-ups, work projects, and daily job responsibilities. It's easy to blame oneself when things don't go as planned. While it's crucial to hold ourselves accountable, it's equally important to maintain perspective. A business concept can simply be ill-timed or fail to align with market needs. Sometimes, things just don't work out.

5. **Embrace the Capacity for Growth**. In a start-up with limited resources and no one to delegate to, individuals are required to take on diverse roles. This is why I believe it's essential for every business professional to spend time working with a small business. It keeps you humble and grounded in reality. For instance, although my initial role was related to strategy and marketing, I had to broaden my contributions to encompass operations, direct sales, and even driving a 26' delivery truck.

Are You Growing Professionally?

As I reflected on these insights, a significant question came to mind—one that we should all ask ourselves:

> **"What professional risks are you taking that have the potential for failure?"**

Genuinely exploring this question will reveal opportunities for learning and growth. Even though our aversion to risk may increase as we age, the inherent connection between failure and learning remains unchanged.

So, go ahead and embrace professional risks! It can be as simple as taking on a new project, acquiring a new skill, or applying for a position in a different department within your company. And just like when you were learning to ride a bike, it's okay to stumble and fall. We all experience setbacks. What matters is that when you encounter failure, you rise again, take a moment to heal your wounds, learn from the experience, and persevere.

Learning from Laziness

I have been approached by younger project managers who are curious about what it takes to successfully lead large projects and programs. To their surprise, I often suggest that they consider embracing the concept of laziness. Now, I must admit that I am having a little fun with the term "lazy," but in all seriousness, there is a valuable lesson to be learned from it.

If you consult a thesaurus for the antonyms of laziness, you will find words such as hard-working, earnest, persistent, and tireless. These words accurately describe the majority of project managers I know. In virtually any initiative, you can safely assume that the project manager is deeply involved. They put in long hours, solve problems, lead meetings, take on additional responsibilities, and ensure that all the work is completed, even if they have to do it themselves. In short, project managers are notoriously bad at being lazy—it simply isn't in our nature.

This realization is crucial. Sometimes, our strengths can become our weaknesses. I firmly believe that this insight is at the heart of what holds many project managers back from advancing to higher levels in their careers.

As projects grow in scope, it becomes increasingly difficult for a single project manager to fill in all the gaps. There are only so many hours in a day. The approach of rolling up one's sleeves and "getting things done" falls apart when there is an overwhelming amount of work to be completed. If project managers persist in trying to do everything themselves, they either burn out or the project fails.

Transitioning from personally executing all the work to motivating others to do it is one of the most challenging shifts a project manager can make. This is where learning from laziness can prove helpful.

The Lesson of Laziness

Learning from laziness does not mean lounging around all day doing nothing. It means being attentive to that little voice in your head that occasionally questions, "Do I really have to do that?" or says, "I have better things to do," or even whispers, "I need a break." These subtle cues, which many busy project managers often ignore, can guide you toward enhancing the quality and impact of your work.

Practice actively acknowledging these signals from your "inner-laziness" voice. Once you become aware of them, the next step is to determine when and how to take positive action. Here are some common actions to consider:

- Delegate the task or action to others.
- Allow people to take ownership of issues, even if it means they might fail or miss a minor deadline. Such experiences can be instructive and prevent the recurrence of similar issues.
- Request additional resources when needed.
- Avoid doing other people's work for them, and don't hesitate to tactfully address missed deadlines or commitments.
- Schedule time to step away from daily project activities to think and work strategically.
- Remember that it's okay to take breaks and recharge. A little rest and relaxation can help you stay on top of your game and minimize the risk of burnout.

The Lesson in Leadership

Even when I share these suggestions, I often receive responses like, "Sure, I'd like to delegate more, but the other team members can't do things as well as me." To that, I say—you have to let go! People will never excel or even surpass you if you don't give them the opportunity. Remember, leadership isn't about you; it's about developing the abilities of the people around you. I guarantee that, more often than not, you will be amazed by the results when you encourage others to take on new responsibilities and grow.

•

ABOUT THE AUTHOR

Jon Hanley

Jon is a project management professional with over 23 years of business experience spanning PMO, project management, consulting, marketing, innovation, information technology, and shared services.

Throughout his career, he has led strategic initiatives at 7-Eleven, Best Buy, Procter & Gamble, as an independent consultant, and on a variety of start-ups and small businesses including Sparkten Partners, Lonely Crates, Thinstaff, and several others. Jon's career includes two expatriate assignments in Latin America and an assignment in Silicon Valley.

His education and accreditations include:

- Master of Business Administration (MBA), Marketing Focus, Xavier University, Cincinnati, Ohio
- Bachelor of Science, Computer Information Systems, Indiana University, Bloomington, Indiana
- Project Management Professional (PMP), Project Management Institute

www.ingramcontent.com/pod-product-compliance
Lightning Source LLC
Chambersburg PA
CBHW072305290526
45794CB00002B/541

* 9 7 9 8 8 5 1 0 2 3 1 6 3 *